In July 2006 British Diplomat Caroline Jaine volunteered to work in Iraq. As a 36-year-old mother of three, who had rarely been parted from her family, she knew she would face unique challenges. This is the story of Caroline's struggles as a female civilian in a war zone. It highlights an extraordinary time during the occupation – those 100 days in Basra Palace were perhaps some of the most volatile and uncertain as the coalition fumbled with a plan for a better Basra and the beginnings of an exit strategy - but Caroline's story is also a touching, personal account of these time and a thoroughly entertaining read.

CAROLINE JAINE

A BETTER BASRA

Searching for Strategy and Sanity in Iraq

Askance Publishing

www.askance-publishing.com

ISBN 978-1-4477-1487-3

Askance Publishing, 152 Blinco Grove, Cambridge, CB1 7TT

With thanks to my father and my husband, both wordsmiths themselves, who provided tireless amounts of proofreading and endless encouragement.

Thanks to my children for their love, and my mother for the inspiration she continues to provide although she is gone.

This story is dedicated to Saman and Assaf who I shared laughs with, who moved me in very different ways with their stories, and who both lost their lives not long after I left Basra Palace.

"If a path to the better there be, it begins with a full look at the worst" - Thomas Hardy

Introduction

June 2010

A few weeks ago I joined about 70 others at the QEII Conference Centre opposite Westminster Abbey in Central London. Together we shared stories, some cried, all laughed, and some simply gazed into the distance. A diverse range of civil servants and consultants, we had one thing in common — we had all served in Iraq at some stage between 2003 and 2009. This was the first time we had ever been gathered together to talk about the successes and failures of our Iraq experience — and the first time many of us had felt listened to. Our hosts and facilitators were Sir John Chilcot and his colleagues, who made up the Iraq Inquiry — and I thank them for providing the opportunity to reflect.

I was only in Iraq for 100 days and next to veterans of years I felt somehow that my experience was inadequate and perhaps that I had over-dramatised it in part - but I was wrong. I soon understood that in the context of the six years that Britain and her allies occupied Iraq, the short time that I had been there, had been quite exceptional in terms of danger — and not least, frustration. There was a realisation too that the civilian effort was often forgotten about and - as I found out first hand as a government Press Officer - was of no real interest to the media. Civilian presence in Iraq was after all dwarfed by the military.

It is for this reason that in June 2010, I searched my hard-drive for the part -finished story of my time in Iraq that I had hastily scrawled a year or so ago and bottom-drawered for future generations of Jaines. But I see now that the story of an ordinary civilian in extraordinary times should be heard by more and not lost. The mere few months I spent living in Iraq proved to be a huge catalyst for change in me, both personally and professionally — but it has taken me several years to realise that I have an interesting story to tell and that I needn't be shy of telling it.

I have written and blogged about freedom of expression — but I now understand that I have been my own worst censor. I joined the Foreign Office in my mid twenties and even as a fledgling diplomat, I bought into the culture that one just didn't write about one's experiences. It just wasn't cricket. The likes of Craig Murray and Christopher Meyer were held up as examples of how NOT to behave, yet many of us would scuttle up to Waterstones on Trafalgar Square to buy their words (core reading for those about to be posted to Washington or Uzbekistan).

I realise of course that I am no Murray, I am no Meyer. I am not about to shine a spotlight on a controversial human rights issue nor offer jaded insight into British/US relations (although maybe a fleeting glimpse on the latter). In Iraq, I was neither an Ambassador nor High Priestess. I was just a woman in a warzone. A mother of three, with honourable - if possibly naïve - intentions, separated from her loved ones for the first time in 13 years and thrown into a world of mortars, rockets and defence correspondents. I am not claiming that I was anything but average. I never saved anyone's life with my bare hands, nor did I patch up a wounded soldier under mortar attack. I didn't crumble, I didn't shine, but I did operate reasonably well in extraordinary and life threatening circumstances and I'm sure that being a female of the species helped me to some extent.

There is another reason for writing this – one which may well be revealed by the Iraq Inquiry – and that is that many civilians are ill-prepared for sharing life in a military theatre.

On a "Hostile Territories" course we were shown real life videos of captives being beheaded, we were chased around woodland by armed men, and mopped up fake blood from the spurting wounds of convincing actors. But it is a bit like reading books on parenthood in preparation for becoming a mum - it is difficult to know exactly how you will behave when the responsibility is with you, when it is actually yours. The more exposure and training you can get before deploying on such an assignment, the better. Reading briefings, going on political courses, and attending meetings are all good — but nothing really prepares you for the experience of living in fear, of co-habiting with the culture of uniform, of "compound" mentality - nor of what to expect from yourself as "normal" when exposed to hyper-stress or physical danger. It is hoped that this account proves to be relaxed and entertaining, but also a useful preparation for anyone (perhaps particularly women) considering volunteering for civilian assignment in a war zone - and I can't help but think of Afghanistan as I write this.

It should be noted however, that as we nibbled polite sandwiches (and some of us gnashed teeth) with our Inquiry friends at the QEII Centre, Sir John quite rightly observed that everyone in the room had a very different story to tell. Those in Maysan and Kirkuk experienced a very different civvy Iraq than those stuck in the bureaucratic hub that was Baghdad. Some felt isolated and frustrated at the lack of ability to meet Iraqis — others enjoyed regular outside contact and a high level of responsibility. Some had witnessed violence first-hand; others had enjoyed their mission from the Embassy bar. Much depended on where you were, when you were in Iraq and more often the personalities you worked with. One thing that can be said is that it was an experience that none of us will forget.

Writing this account is made easier as I kept a diary whilst I was in Iraq and wrote a weekly email to friends back in England. Most of my diplomatic assignments have had real-time reflections scribbled throughout, perhaps in the hope that one day it would be of some interest, even to an inquisitive great-grandchild who might grapple with their own nomadic tendencies and like to see where it all came from.

Glancing back a few years, before we arrive at the inevitable "what-the-fuck-were-you-doing-in-Iraq" question (one I was and still am frequently faced with), I would like to share a diary entry written in Colombo, Sri Lanka in September 2001:

> *Last week I was chatting on the phone to my mate Lauren about progress on the photography book we are working on, when I absent-mindedly turned on the TV and saw a plane flying into the World Trade Centre in New York. Twenty minutes later Lauren and her boyfriend (who had no electricity in their own home due to the daily black-outs), were sitting on our sofa watching the carnage going on in America as if it were the latest Bruce Willis action movie – it somehow didn't seem real. We silently sipped cold beers as our generator belched black smoke and provided a background roar for the disturbing images of the deaths of thousands as the Twin Towers collapsed before our very eyes. Next we saw the smashed Pentagon and dusty, fraught American civil servants in blind panic.*

> *Theories are bouncing around, but America seemed to have made up its mind pretty much straight away. Islamic Fundamentalists. I suppose when you have the likes of Bin Laden threatening to crush The West almost on a weekly basis, it is not surprising that he may be a chief suspect. And with people like Mr S Hussein allegedly saying "jolly good job, whoever did*

it" and the media showing pictures of Palestinians throwing a party in Jerusalem to celebrate (even though the pictures were allegedly taken a few years ago for another occasion), the world seems quite happy to blame Muslims. Something inside me hopes that they are wrong. I hope that it was American white supremacists, perhaps put out by the interracial nature of the Big Apple. Or that it was school kids from Texas who masterminded this mass murder after a lifetime of being bullied and collecting guns. I have to take my hat off to the organisation of it; it's quite an achievement to get two large passenger jets to crash into one specific spot in the heart of New York. It puts the recent Tamil Tiger attack on the airport here in the shade. But alas whoever did it has not owned up to it, which to me is the absolute evil of evils. I might get it if you have a cause to highlight, if you are fighting FOR something, if you give a reason for attacking your so-called enemy, however harsh. But the only reason for this seems to be just "wanting people dead". I don't think it will harm the economy so much, if that was the plan. If the plan was to polarise America and drag out fundamentalist evil in the USA, then that seems to be working. They are demanding blood. I honestly don't think that the death of Bin Laden would be enough for the people from the land of plenty. I think they honestly want to see a few thousand innocent civilians dead in the same way that they have suffered. And Mr Bush is massing his troops and planes and boats and missiles and aiming them at Afghanistan, which surely has little left to bomb really. I am sure that they will miss Bin Laden who is probably sitting in a James Bond style underground cavern of steel or floating above us in a space ship quietly chuckling, in his leather chair, stroking his pussy cat with a scarred hand – if he even exists at all.

In the 1990's the hip-hop song "The Revolution Will Not Be Televised" by KRS-One was a favourite of mine. How wrong they were, it is unavoidable today. The suffering of the American people is being pumped into our heads every second of the day via CNN, World Service and good old tabloid Sky News who are desperate to keep the momentum going on this story and wishing Mr Bush would hurry up and attack the Afghans now so their audience figures are maintained. And via the internet, alternative stories are being circulated; that of media misrepresentation (of the Palestinian people), that of the plight of the Afghan people, and of the ego of Mr Bush. I wonder if we would think the world a different place if other disasters were as personalised as this? With face to face accounts from Kurdish refugees or accounts from those who rescued people with their bare hands from the rubble of an Iranian earthquake? What is clear and what almost seems to be desired by many is world war three – the West versus Islam.

Some Sri Lankans here are going mad about Nostradamus and I can't tell you the number of extracts from that drunken madman's ramblings that have ended up in my email inbox this week. Odd that a country which won't make a move unless the stars are auspiciously aligned, has spent the last 19 years in civil war. And they, like the Israelis, align themselves with the Americans and say that they have personal experience with similar terrorist attacks. But no, actually this is very, very different. The terrorism they have known has a voice, a voice which comes from poverty, violence, and oppression and - on a day-to-day level – from a lack of respect and lack of tolerance of diversity. America's crime has been arrogance. It's like the smart, strong, rich kid at school getting a good kicking by a handful of misfits. But it is still just wrong.

Everyone's emotions have been highly charged. I wonder how our one member of staff who is a Muslim feels having the finger pointed at her, as part of the global Islamic Nation. I certainly feel no differently towards the many Muslim visa applicants who this week have produced more forged documents than you could wave a stick at, but do I detect a note of condemnation in my colleague's voices?

The day after we saw "US UNDER ATTACK" on our TVs, a man broke into the High Commission grounds and - with tears in his eyes - attempted to lower our flag to half mast. We do, of course, like with everything, have to wait for authority from Her Majesty to lower a flag, but he did not understand. It was only after Big John the Visa Manager had wrestled him to the ground that we learned that he was the Methodist minister from the church down the street. The US Embassy next door lowered their flag soon after this incident and on getting the flash telegram from London we did the same to ours, to the Minister's relief.

In the days following the September 11th attack, it was clear to me that something equally nasty would befall, well, Afghanistan, clearly. And so it did. But that is another tale for another time.

The Invasion of Iraq

I was still living in Sri Lanka when Britain joined America's attack on Iraq on 20th March 2003. The build up to the invasion was uncomfortable. Everyone at the High Commission was told to buckle-down on security and we learned how to check our vehicles for car bombs and varied our routes to work, whilst we saw many of our US colleagues in the Embassy next door simply fly back to America. Two days before the invasion I wrote in my diary: *"We all wait with baited breath to see if Saddam & Sons leave Iraq in 48 hours. I think I know the answer already"*.

The signal that the war in Iraq had started came at 3am on 20th March 2003, with the arrival of the Sri Lankan Special Task Force outside our home. Two of them were asleep across the barrels of their loaded weapons in the garage the next morning. We were told to keep the children away from school and although I went to work at the High Commission, as soon as we learned there was a large demonstration planned outside the US Embassy that day, all staff were sent home early.

Our regular guards were two Tamil cousins who argued day and night, but we liked them very much and they played cricket with the children in the garage and on the street outside our house. Unarmed as they were, they suddenly found themselves redundant as guards and were demoted to making tea for the new soldiers who shared their space. The addition of the soldiers was unwelcome all round as they made us feel *more* vulnerable not less. Dotted around the wealthy suburbs of Colombo the additional "security" flagged up every British and American diplomatic household in town – good information for any potential enemy. My assignment on the tropical island of serendipity was about to change – and all because of the War on Terror that was happening many miles away.

On my birthday 11 days later, with a tongue firmly in my cheek, I wrote: *"We haven't taken Baghdad yet. The Visa*

Section at work remains closed in case someone brings a pile of Semtex cunningly disguised as a visa application form".

Twenty two days after the invasion, whilst taking a break with my family in India, we heard news that the war in Iraq appeared to have come to an end. Peter, to whom I was married at the time, had been growing a beard in protest since the war began, and enjoyed having a roadside bucket-and-blade shave in Jaipur to mark the occasion. Once we arrived in Delhi after a hot trek across Rajasthan in a jeep, we soaked up some air conditioning and cable news channels. On Indian TV, we snatched our first glimpses of the scenes of jubilation in Iraq as Saddam's face was torn down and torn up. I remember there were green parrots on the window ledge as I looked out across the city of Delhi. I flopped onto the bed in the hotel room and wrote something in my notebook that makes me smile (or is that grimace?) when I read it over today: *"I hope things will start to improve for the Iraqi people. I am sure that not all of them are terribly impressed with the UK/US occupation of Iraq, but our propaganda is reliably informing us that the British troops are especially lovely to the locals".*

Back in Sri Lanka, back at work, it became apparent that the British were not exactly flavour of the month in Colombo. Pressure was mounting, not least because my health was failing, but also because one of my colleagues was under investigation for corruption and visa fraud which was making big news in the Sri Lankan press. My tendency to mingle with Sri Lankans rather than other ex-pats, meant that things got pretty tough socially. Not only was I being asked about my colleague and his sex-for-visas scandal exposé (the tabloid take on it), but I was being put on the spot over British action in Iraq, especially by my Muslim friends. One friend, an eminent peace-loving intellectual and a great artist who had recently taken up wearing the hijab, I felt hardly able to look in the eye. As a diplomat I was obliged to toe the line. Well, quite clearly I couldn't be seen to be criticizing the government I represented, but frankly I was often lost for words, so I began to slink back into the safe ex-pat zones of places like the Hilton and

Colombo Swimming Club and hide amongst the fair-skinned folk. Hell, I even went to the American Marine Ball in search of allies - a mistake not to be repeated - we sat with a Netherlands crowd and nearly got thrown out for sniggering during the singing of the Star Spangled Banner.

My mood was not cheered any by a man named Perera, who somehow got hold of my government email address and sent me obscene photos of dead Iraqi children. Not once or twice, but every single day for weeks. Finally our IT people were able to block him, but not before the disturbing images of the charred and mutilated little bodies had left an imprint on my mind. Needless to say, by the time I left Sri Lanka towards the end of that year, I was exhausted, fed up and more than ready for some leave away from work.

Righting

A few years later, after a reasonably unsatisfactory break I found myself back in Whitehall working as a speech writer and researcher attached to the Foreign Office Press Office.

For the first time the work professionally challenged me and a love of disciplined writing overwhelmed me. Working alongside two talented and eloquent speech writers, Sarah and John, my skills were honed. Sarah was perhaps the most graceful, stylish diplomat I have had the pleasure to work with and John didn't look a day older than he did when I worked with him nine years prior to that in the Security Policy Department. The job introduced me to the "Big Picture Foreign Office" and between us we flitted across a rainbow of foreign policy issues. Working from home mainly, I wrote about and researched Morocco, Modern Diplomacy, Iran and EU Enlargement. I wrote speeches for Ministers attending Jewish dinners, Trade Associations and Memorial services. No subject too big or too small. It was a steep learning curve beginning with my inaugural written speech for Dr Kim Howells, which was utterly atrocious and had to be re-written a hundred times, and ending with a more successful attempt to write a speech about South Africa for Margaret Beckett on one of her first engagements as Foreign Secretary. John changed the title on the door to our lavish office, which overlooked St James Park, to read "Speech Righters" and I set about networking with speechwriters across Whitehall and getting more media attention for our carefully crafted words. The speeches we wrote were rousing (well they were when I read them to myself in my head) and I started to believe in what I was writing. One of the biggest challenges was getting a Blackburn Rovers reference into each of Jack Straw's anecdotes. I even joined the fan club of the football team, such was my dedication! It was without doubt my most enjoyable assignment in the Foreign Office and for the first time I felt perhaps dangerously close to having a sense of purpose. Maybe things were too good on that apple cart.

Then, at a routine security vetting interview, questions turned to my support for British Foreign Policy. My time then dominated by the promotion of British ideals, I was able to offer my support confidently. But something irked me that needed to be got off my chest. I hesitated. An advocate of "honesty is the only policy", my gaze lowered and my less than 100% support for the government's decision to go into Iraq was tentatively communicated to the vetting officer interviewing me. Noting the edginess in my own frankness, he laughed. You and everyone else! he said, and nodded as he ticked his boxes and issued me with my security clearance.

Well, I shouldn't be surprised. It was reasonably well known that a legal advisor at the Foreign & Commonwealth Office (FCO) advised Blair against action in Iraq, and some felt that the relationship between No. 10 and the FCO was sliding downhill. Robin Cook was not the best loved Foreign Secretary by FCO staff - I even cursed at him once, by mistake when he bashed into me in a corridor - but we were with him on Iraq.

The security interview transpired to be an enormous turning point for me. It was confirmation that many of my colleagues felt as I did, and confirmation that this was not necessarily a damming sign of disloyalty. And perhaps a naïve belief in the stirring speeches I was writing also played a part in the decision I was about to make.

Iraq began to play on my mind. A couple of colleagues in the Press Office had actually been there and I started to ask them about it. Hell, I thought, if so many of my colleagues felt so strongly about Iraq, why weren't they queuing up to go? Surely us quiet objectors should be offering to support the British Government with their noble reconstruction efforts? But it was well known that the Foreign Office had a recruitment problem for Iraq, which was compounded by the very short tour lengths for volunteers – most stayed only six months. There was a feeling that those who would volunteer for Iraq had already done so. The pool was becoming depleted.

So, why not me? The chance of a successful application was clearly high. It would be good for my career (allegedly). And I would be helping the good, suffering people of Iraq.

The seed was sown, and with a reputation for glossing over harsh realities – the actual danger of being in a frontline war-zone was entirely overlooked by me. I needed to put my money where my mouth was and my mouth where the money was. A very short time later notice was received of my successful bid for the position of Press & Public Affairs/Economic/Political Officer at the British Embassy Office in Basra. I thought I was being very clever picking Basra over Baghdad. Much safer, everyone told me.

I worked on speeches pretty much right up until my departure for Iraq in the summer of 2006, and fitted in a handful (but not nearly enough) of training courses and briefings. In the spring, Mr Straw was cosying up to Condoleezza Rice in Blackburn and the media were preoccupied with irrelevant aspects in their relationship, like the fact that Jack slept on the floor of the plane they shared, whilst Condoleezza stretched out in luxury. It signified Britain's relationship with the US they said, although she was reportedly quite charmed by his gesture. Snakes on a Plane.

John was grappling with speeches for both Condi's visit and a key-note speech on Iran. I spent my days finding connections between Rice's native Birmingham, Alabama, where Straw had recently been her guest and Straw's constituency in Lancashire. Hours of Google interrogation revealed that cotton was the only tangible link between the two places and I cunningly "wove" it into the speech (a-hem). But, although unconnected, everything I did was beginning to be seen through the prism of Iraq.

I learned that Condeleezza came from an unusual background for a Republican. She had experienced a terror attack as a child of eight - the famous bombing of the Sixteenth Street Baptist Church by white supremacists. I couldn't help but wonder how this affected her. Perhaps this drove her to advocate such a heavy-handed response to perceived threats (Iraq again). Here in Britain, she was confronted by angry crowds as an aggressor herself and the Stop The War Coalition put an end to her planned visit to a mosque. Ironically my little brother was one of the thousands of anti-War-on-Terror students who turned out to boo and chant as Ms Rice arrived. She did manage to get to Ewood Park of course - home of the beloved Blackburn Rovers where she delivered a nice lecture on liberal democracy, with no mention of football at all.

Shortly before I moved to Southern Iraq, and to the astonishment of many Foreign Office staff, Jack Straw was relieved of his post and Margaret Beckett became the first female Foreign Secretary. The word "token" springs to mind for more than one reason (I have good reason to be a bitch here – I was to meet her in Basra a few months later).

In those weeks leading up to my departure, one challenge was coping with John's humorous mumbling through the partition wall in our office. All was going bad in Basra and John promised me that I would surely die if I went there. He emailed me links to articles that backed up this theory. But my trainer on the Hostile Territories course seemed to think Basra was quite a luxurious spot and referred to it as "Baz-bitha" on account of the compound swimming pool, choice of bars and sunny climate.

I trained alongside an old friend, Colin, who was heading out to Kabul and I was feeling quite smug about my posting. The plan was for Peter and the kids to move to Kuwait – with schooling provided by the well reputed English School of Kuwait, and the Embassy would provide accommodation not far from some friends who we knew from our posting to Slovakia a few years earlier. There was also a chance that I could visit from Basra at weekends – as it was only an hour and a half drive north of Kuwait City. It was far from ideal for the kids to be away from their mother, but everyone seemed excited by another overseas adventure and it meant that whilst I was deploying to Iraq they could initially spend time with their grandmother in South Africa. Besides, I would only be there for six months. That was the plan anyway.

Another colleague who was convinced that an assignment to Basra was a good idea was the FCO's Arabic Spokesman, Jason. I had met him a few times in the Press Office and was happy to be working with someone with the same cynical sense of humour as my own. Just days before departure, the two of us were plodding up and down Victoria Street like a couple of distressed polar bears in a zoo, in a blind attempt to locate The Government Stabilisation Unit, which at the time was housed on the third floor of a tatty office block (we did find it in the end). The mild English sunshine lifted our spirits as we laughed at our ineptitude at finding the office which, to be fair, was about as easy to spot as Platform 9¾ at Kings Cross. We hoped that we would be able to find the Foreign Office Compound at Basra Palace, and even joked that we might get lost on the streets of Basra - little did we know we wouldn't even set foot on them.

Other training included economic reporting, political reporting, meeting journalists, attending a Downing Street press briefing at the Foreign Press Association and meeting colleagues at the BBC World Service Trust. The charming Gerry told a roomful of would-be press officers set for Eastern Europe, Asia and America, entertaining stories from his own experiences and what to expect from the job. His soft Irish tones were easy on the ear, but despite being ludicrously and foolishly keen, I still wasn't sure how I was going to set about refocusing the world's media onto development and reconstruction and away from military tales in Basra, as was the task.

On the Hostile Territories residential course we learnt how to be good hostages (i.e. ones that stay alive the longest); how to tell if someone pointing a gun at you knows how to use it and from what range; and we learnt about IEDs (improvised explosive devices) and rockets and mortars and how to run away quickly or how to throw oneself on the ground - and with the use of some realistic dud thuds I did just that. We were taught how to communicate over radios, how to cross-deck in and out of armoured vehicles and – importantly - how to administer emergency first aid - and I was ludicrously keen to try that too. Some of the things we were taught were potential life savers - like checking for hideous amounts of bleeding behind the knees of a partially crushed driver and the importance of ensuring a casualty keeps their head perfectly still to avoid neck damage. One moment that sticks in my mind is jumping onto the bonnet of a smoking vehicle rather over enthusiastically screaming, "don't move!" at the mock victim. I think I thought I was in a Tarantino movie.

It was an intensive but fun experience and although our trainers remained tough and aloof, by the end of it, we all felt like friends. Everyone passed the "physical test" which our small team achieved by carting Colin around the grounds of the Oxfordshire conference centre on a stretcher.

With some exposure to stressful situations, my ability to cope under pressure had been tested to a certain extent. My main concern was my natural curiosity and a desire to witness the full story - often with complete disregard for my own safety (I may have made a good journalist!). A few years earlier, anti-government riots in the part of Colombo where we lived saw tear gas canisters fired into our street. My security guard and driver stopped me from joining a potentially dangerous crowd, and my housekeeper and I were forced to watch the commotion from a roof top balcony. In Sri Lanka I also dealt with traumatic deaths of consular clients, was chased by mental patients around Angoda Asylum and spent time at Jaffna hospital with land mine victims. I knew myself to be fairly good natured and calm in dangerous and unsavoury circumstances.

We said our goodbyes, the trainers disappeared, and I went to collect my children from school.

I have never enjoyed the school playground much, even as a child, but I won't forget quite how much of an alien I felt that Friday in June 2006, waiting for my eldest son, Billy and my daughter, Daisy to appear after a week away from them.

The English sun was warm and my head was still echoing from the sound of exploding duds and the shouts of mercenaries. I stood apart from the crowd, wearing my brand new desert boots and let my kids run into my arms. It had really only been a week – already the longest I had been apart from them - and with a tear in my eye and some odd glances from "normal" mums, I wondered how I would cope in Iraq. It was a going to be a test indeed.

Bye-Bye Bourn

"I did sit down with them at one point and I explained that this was going to be extremely difficult and it was possible that the thing could go against me" - Tony Blair, in The Sun, 18 April 2003, on telling his children he could lose his job over the Iraq war

So, aside from saying goodbye to my three beautiful children and my husband, not to forget an enjoyable and exciting job with a daily healthy discourse of foreign policy issues, I was also leaving behind a group of good friends in the village of Bourn where I lived. We were united by a tendency for late nights (usually Thursdays), a taste for good wine (actually cheap wine would do), and having children of a similar age. We all felt there was something that set us apart from other playground mums. I can't put my finger on it - a varied bunch of women, some of us have lived abroad - some as far away as Scotland - we are teachers, property developers, school governors, home owners – perhaps nothing out of the ordinary, but the fact that we had a stuffed moose head as our mascot (which is generally brought out at auspicious gatherings) should ring alarm bells perhaps.

Looking back, I think the girls thought my going to Iraq was part of some (early) mid life crisis that I had to "get out of my system," much like the X-Factor audition the year before. Erm…. I didn't win that one, by the way. The collapse of my marriage when I returned to Bourn 100 days later also supported the mid-life crisis theory.

It was clear that some in the village thought my decision a selfish act, one that would endanger me and take me away from my children. Although I totally failed to take on board the danger aspect until right at the end, I really thought, particularly for my daughter, that a tremendous example would be set - stepping out of the traditional female role and showing them that anything was possible. There were no qualms about how right it was for Peter to stop working and be a full time carer for the kids, or about sending them to a

29

new school in Kuwait. As a family we had done this kind of thing before – and we were famous for our ability to adapt. But we had spent the previous few years in this sleepy village and although the inhabitants had heard about our nomadic lifestyle (I gave talks about Sri Lanka at the village school), they hadn't really witnessed it before and to them it was an extraordinary thing to do.

One thing that was clearly underestimated was just how worried people were going to be about me. On my return to the village that winter, I would bump into virtual strangers in the local shop who would warmly welcome me home and visibly sigh with relief that I was safe.

But it was really nothing compared to the worry those closest to me experienced. Not unjustifiably I was called selfish on my return, but hats off to my mother (who worried if the cat went missing for more than half an hour at a time) and my children, who, through it all displayed courage and affection for me. Memories of delicately telling my daughter that I would be "spending time in Iraq" whilst we were living in Kuwait: standing in the kitchen in our cottage, cooking a stir-fry, she doing maths homework at the kitchen table, me throwing in the soy sauce. "Cool!" she said, "Am I allowed to tell my friends?" I never overlooked the fact that they were without their mother for a spell, but I did shield them from the worst – and I have made it up to them in terms of time spent ever since – not least as a single mum on my return!

My girl-friends in Bourn were extra special to me because I never felt any good at making friends with women. Even, at school (when I bothered to go), I lacked the ability to be part of a close female clique. My only friends were lone soldiers, like me, and I never felt part of a crowd in my younger years. And later, as a working mum abroad, I was never joined the tennis playing, coffee morning, stitches and bitches gang. My poor husband was faced with some dreadful women when he attempted to join a spouses' meeting once – he wisely took up playing cricket and long distance running instead. The fish-out-of-water phenomenon usually worked well for me, and as a family we thrived on the periphery of ex-pat communities, but moving to a small British village community was one of the biggest challenges of my life. So to find a bunch of ready-made female misfits already well established was a treasure and without doubt it was my contact with this bunch of women during my Basra days that kept me sane. It kept lightness and humour in my heart and it meant that one foot was kept permanently in another reality – one that was as solid and supportive as a rock.

Q8

The first test of friendship was at Heathrow airport. Although all that was needed was carefully packed (sleeping bag, whistle, compass, knife, plastic bag, even a mosquito net) I had completely forgotten the one thing that in those days would get me into Iraq – my Ministry of Defence ID card. Luckily my friend Louise came to the rescue by breaking into my house, retrieving the pass from its cunningly hidden location on the coat hooks and tearing down the M11 motorway to reach me with minutes to spare. Not a great start, but one that at least distracted me from a potentially heart-wrenching and tearful goodbye to the family.

I enjoy travelling on my own, I always have done. Maybe because my life is (was) usually pretty crowded with other people, whether it was work colleagues, my friends, my kids, friends of my kids, kids of my friends - our house always seemed full. Suddenly I was alone and feeling all purposeful and dynamic – the messiah complex in full flow. Usually a nervous flyer, there was rising excitement as the plane flew over the sandy deserts of Kuwait and I was overcome with an urgent need to know what the Iraq landscape would actually look like. I still didn't know at that stage what method of transport would ultimately take me to Basra. The usual route was to fly in an RAF Hercules to Baghdad, then back down to Basra, but rumour had it that the road route was considered potentially safe enough to use again. Such arrangements were not discussed over email or phone; it would be a case of wait and see.

On arrival in Kuwait I was met, as arranged, next to the coffee shop at the airport by someone from the Embassy. We had been told to keep a low profile at the airport as it was being watched by "hostile forces", so I left my union flag shorts behind and wore my hijab (this is a joke, I own neither). But, in light of this advice, it was a surprise to see a private from the US Army in the welcome lounge bearing a large sign with US ARMY IRAQ TROOPS writ large. He was gathering young shaven-headed men from another flight. Well, it was not exactly low profile. A classic American mistake.

My colleague discreetly whisked me off to the special section at the British Embassy tasked with supporting our offices in Iraq. They did everything from flight arranging to buying goods unavailable in Iraq. In fact every time someone passed through they were invariably asked to take something from one Management Officer to another - and in time people would learn to hate my bundles of newspapers! I remember offering to take hundreds of long life batteries to Basra and having a chuckle with my colleagues in Kuwait about what the Management Officer in Basra might be using them for. Well, come on, even a diplomat is allowed a filthy mind from time to time. Karma got me – the batteries weighed a ton, and I regretted my over-confident and rather brash offer to carry the lot.

During my brief stop in Kuwait, apart from the batteries, I was issued with a helmet and some body armour that stunk of somebody else's sweat. Once outside the embassy, beyond the finely watered shady gardens and in the dusty heat on the road outside, I tried the lot on and groaned. This was going to be the best weight-loss plan ever – wearing a snug body-hugging 12kg worth of body armour in 50 degree heat – not to mention the hat strapped tightly under my chin! It was quite understandable that some people slipped out the ceramic plates for comfort - I felt like a cricketer going out to bat in my dad's oversized pads. I even pondered the merits of an armoured box for the men in such circumstances.

The armour and batteries were stashed in the back of a 4x4 jeep and my next mission was to zoom across town to visit the apartment that Peter and kids would be living in whilst I roughed it in Iraq. It was a sizeable three bed-roomed and many bath-roomed space with elegant furniture and even interesting art on the walls. Housed in a plush block where other Embassy staff lived it felt like it would more than suffice. The communal swimming pool caught my eye – the kids were all brilliant swimmers and would love it. I nodded my approval, but didn't want to stay too long. I had already begun to block any thought of my loved ones from my mind in order to focus on what could be a perilous journey ahead. My Embassy colleague had just informed me that they were going to try and get me into Basra by road. It was the word "try" that I had problems with.

Border Crossing

The same 4x4 vehicle drove me for about 45 minutes out of Kuwait City through an exceptionally featureless landscape. Just sand, dust and flatness - nothing more. This is the same road that Saddam's tanks had driven down on 2 August 1990 when they took Kuwait (with ease), only to be driven back in the direction that I was travelling some six months later when the UN liberated Kuwait during Operation Desert Storm. My driver pointed to a small hill covered with tufts of grass to his left and said "Desert Storm....over there" and although I made interested "ahhhh" and "ooohhhh" sounds, I didn't really get what he was pointing out. I had been living in Israel at the beginning of the Gulf War, under the threat of the dreaded Scud missiles and the friendly Patriots that were sent to intercept them. I had avidly followed Desert Storm on TV, but 15 years on in Kuwait this relic of the Gulf War felt disappointing – simply a few flat and lifeless grassy knolls. Besides, I didn't want to get into all that, I was anxious to get to the border and onto Iraqi soil; the whole Gulf War thing was a different story that I didn't want to be troubled by right then. I had in my mind Saddam's statue being pulled down and the British soldiers chucking out sweeties to smiling Iraqi kids. People throwing flowers onto tanks. Democratic elections, that kind of thing.

We waited at the border for some time. It wasn't quite clear when the situation was supposed to "get dangerous" or when to expect to be afraid, but I decided to chain-smoke in case it had started and I had missed it. Luckily my travelling companion was a guy named Chris. He worked as an administrator at the Embassy Office and was returning to Basra after a rest and recuperation (R&R) break. He answered my questions patiently and was and continued to be, without doubt the most laid back, cool colleague I have ever worked with. An amazing response to his environment considering he was just 22 years old at the time. Apart from Chris and I, there were several others lurking in the desert heat – they were all smoking cigarettes too. There were some other 4x4 vehicles, and a couple of trucks parked up.

There were one or two Portaloos, but no real buildings or semblance of what looked like a border crossing.

Then a small convoy of armoured vehicles arrived. It was our close protection team – eight fully armed men looking every bit as tough as I had been led to believe they would. It was unbelievable that this bunch of heavily tooled up mercenaries had just driven through southern Iraq, risking IEDs, to come and collect gangly young Chris and a slightly nervous mother of three. I was stepping into a movie set, surely? A feeling came creeping over me – one that would be repeated in weeks to come – civilians DIDN'T belong here. How many civvy's did you see on war films? I couldn't think of a single example.

The curt security team were firm yet polite and nestled me into the middle one of the three vehicles, with body armour and helmet now on - falling over my eyes, heart beginning to pound a little faster. The driver was a huge Fijian man amusingly named Penny (I didn't laugh though) who offered a smile and somehow seemed to know straightaway that this was my first time in Iraq. To say I felt safe with them was an understatement. The utter professionalism of those men never failed to impress me throughout my time there.

The border wasn't really a border to speak of, more a dusty car park where we "paused" momentarily rather than stopped. Once across and into Iraq the landscape became more interesting. I began to relax a bit and enjoy it, even take photos on my phone. Arid stretches littered with rusted twists of wreckage and the odd small child amongst derelict brick homes. Chris was so laid back that he fell asleep for most of it. I chatted nervously at first to my protectors who were in constant contact with one another and their base on the radio. The journey lasted a little over an hour, driving pretty quickly along the deserted Tampa Route. We barely passed another vehicle, but once spotted a small convoy of American military in the distance. I was relieved to arrive at what was an enormous military base, stuck in the middle of nowhere. On waking, Chris let me know that we were at

Basra Air Station and still had the most hairy part of our journey ahead of us — getting into the Palace compound in Basra City. I stupidly asked the Fijian why we didn't just keep going and drive on to there. "Too dangerous," he laughed and he dismounted the vehicle and unloaded his clip. Oh. Right.

Arrival at the Palace

Chris must have had a pretty wild R&R because he slept some more, leaving me to pace around in the dirt at the FCO compound on the military base. Everyone I bumped into looked the same – in their 40s (if not 50s), very tanned (if not black), short hair (if not shaven), and bulky (but not fat). I was able to have brief conversations with the ones who stepped out of Portakabins and freight containers for a cigarette. But I don't think I have ever felt greener than in my first few days in Iraq. Everyone around me had a very believable "been there, seen it, done it" look - an expression that I have involuntarily adopted on occasion myself since my return, especially in the context of a sleepy Cambridgeshire village. Lots of hollow laughs when I asked what it was like at the Palace, but also some genuine concern - and my first bout of what-the-fuck-are-you-doing-in-Iraq questions. I felt like SUCH a pillock trying to explain to this cynical bunch that I thought I might be able to do some good in a country that we helped fuck up (see my language was already getting bad around these people). Instead I just shrugged, and said something pathetic like, "I dunno, bored I guess." Honestly. Call myself a diplomat?

After a few hours Chris stirred from his bizarre luxury-armchair-in-a-Red-Sea-freight-container location and managed to get us assigned with a radio and a call sign. This allowed us to scramble a few hundred metres in the searing heat to the Subway sandwich bar and for me to see my first real life soldiers "in theatre".

Here was that movie feeling again, but this time the soldiers, perhaps about a hundred or so of them, were like extras waiting to go on set. I was intrigued about where they had been, what they had done in Iraq so far and where they were off to. What was their day like? Why weren't they at that moment busy "soldiering". I guess even soldiers have lunch breaks or dinner breaks, whatever the time was (I had no idea). These men (and a few women) were three-dimensional human beings – some were glum, some quietly sitting reading, others smiling, joking with animated bellows of

41

hearty laughter. Some were smoking - like I was, AGAIN. Some were munching on fresh Subway sandwiches or drinking coke. They barely glanced up at Chris and me, which surprised me, considering how clearly different and civilian we looked (and felt). I must have been nearly twenty years older than many of them, and by now my linen shirt was soaked a darker shade with sweat; I had beaming, red, exhausted cheeks and was severely squinting from lack of sunglasses. To say I felt self-conscious was an understatement. We had stumbled onto the wrong film set, clearly. They were being filmed by Spielberg, whilst we were in a cheap cable TV documentary about inadequate civil servants.

Many hours later, after more dozing (Chris) and more bewilderment (me), the pair of us, weighed down with body armour, bags, and those damn batteries were shouted into the back of a Merlin helicopter by an airman waving a small, flickering torch in the darkness. *Watch out for the rear rotor, watch out for the rear rotor* I kept telling myself, remembering my training. I tried to follow the quick pace of the body in front of me to keep in line with his path. It was very dark. The blades blew warm dust up into our eyes and did not stop turning – they only touched down for a few minutes, enough time to load and then they were off like a shuttle bus.

The helicopter flew with its lights out so as not to be seen and I could just about make out the outlines of the 20 or so soldiers who were, like me, strapped into their seats. I had been warned that strapping yourself into a Merlin was a tricky operation, but it seemed I had acquired an unlikely skill. I may have been a civilian, and a female one at that, but having had three children and strapped them all into baby, child and booster seats with various buckle configurations – I was better placed than any to fathom the military seat belt situation. It proved no challenge. The first of many examples proving that motherhood was a good preparation for war.

We flew with the flap at the back of the helicopter down so that the rear gunner could precariously perch with his weapon facing any potential threat from the ground.   He was attached to the Merlin by a thin cable, and my maternal instinct wanted to say, "oh do be careful! You could fall if you don't watch out! Are you sure that thing is strong enough?" Not that he would have heard me - the noise was such that his ears were well protected (a little more impressively than my squishy yellow ear plugs from Boots). Another gunner was poised at a side sliding door, opposite me. Apart from soldiers, the space was also packed full of bags, boxes and equipment forming lumpy night-time shapes down the central aisle of the aircraft. As the side gunner turned to flick switches and talk into his very complicated looking headgear, the light from the console revealed an almost childlike face. A teenager, it was clear, and not that much older than my daughter. He turned back, fixed his night sights in front of his eyes and stood ready by his weapon and we lifted off. My tummy lurched in a heady mixture of excitement and fear.

Once we were up in the air, the gentle turbulent sway began to calm me slightly. I caught glimpses of Basra City below and thousands of dots of electric light told me that contrary to the rumour mill, Basrawis had some power at least. It looked like any city, flying over it by night and I wondered how it would look in the daylight – although I understood well why we were now flying under cover of darkness:

Bloody battles were fought on the streets of Basra last night after a British helicopter crashed in the city, reportedly killing four airmen and drawing an Iraqi crowd shouting 'Victory to the Mahdi army'.

At least three British army vehicles were set on fire as the crowd hurled petrol bombs at troops trying to reach the blazing wreckage. Iraqi police officials believed the aircraft had been brought down by a shoulder-fired missile. Four charred bodies were seen inside it, reports said.

Source: Jason Burke and Ned Temko in the Guardian, Sunday May 7 2006

Although deafening, the thudding drum of the helicopter was somehow reassuring. Something about the sheer forward movement of travel makes me feel like I am achieving something, and my confidence grew as every minute passed. However somewhere very deep down a small voice inside me was saying, "Just what the hell are you doing now, you fool?" I told the voice to shut up and reassured it that there was no doubt, I *was* going to have a rich and rewarding experience. I even foolishly told myself that the difference I would be making to the lives of those people down below me in Basra was worth it.

Another thud, this time out of sync with the turning blades and in an instant flash the expression of every fellow passenger was illuminated. They looked bored, tired and showed not a flicker of reaction - unlike my own expression which must have glowed in absolute terror. Chris glanced at me and the soldier sitting next to me shouted in my ear – "it's alright ma'am, it just means they've got a lock on us". Funnily enough, the reassurance didn't really help much. I had heard how counter measures worked - a large flash of heat fired so that anything heat-seeking would be attracted to that rather than the aircraft. But for some reason I wasn't expecting it to make a bang, which to the untrained ear could easily be mistaken for being hit. I was also unprepared for the dramatic twists and turns of evasive flying that followed, which to a stupid person, could also be mistaken for the fact that we had been hit. The only thing keeping me from peeing my pants as we (deliberately) rapidly lost height was the relative calm of the people around me. Chris grinned at me in the darkness, he really was one laid back dude.

The journey was only about ten or fifteen minutes long. The lights vanished and water could be made out very close

44

beneath us, the downdraft from helicopter creating ripples in the blackness. I knew we were nearly there, as the Basra Palace Compound was situated on the banks of the Shatt-Al-Arab waterway.

The Palace itself could not be seen as we landed and disembarked with similar shouts and flickering lights as before. Within minutes a waiting huddle of soldiers on the ground had clambered on board the craft we had just left. Moments later the Merlin was shuddering off into the darkness again, leaving me open mouthed in disbelief that I had been on board such a machine. I felt well and truly part of the war-movie.

We had another short trip in an armoured 4x4 from the military part of the compound to my new home on the FCO side. A Nepalese guard peeped through a hole in a large metal gate and then opened it up and waved us through, smiling. We were taken to the operations room in the basement of one of the Palace buildings, where I was given the key to my pod (a purpose-built reinforced concrete room) by one of the stiff-moustachioed security team. Chris kindly agreed to show me to my room - although it was only a two minute walk, the thought of stumbling around in the pitch dark trying to find my way didn't appeal. Irrational panic was beginning to set in - the prospect of my new key not fitting into the lock and the risk of being stranded outdoors all night loomed. Jittery, I was also vaguely aware that although it was safest to fly at night, night-time was also the most popular time for incoming rocket and mortar attacks. The insistence by the security team that we kept our body armour and helmets on was testament to the danger. But the skies were silent that night.

My key did fit in the lock and Chris bade me goodnight. We had got on very well throughout the journey; he made me laugh - he took the piss out of my new looking desert boots - and although it was four o'clock in the morning I would have loved for him to stay and talk some more. In fact chatting to anyone would have been preferable to the solitude of my room - I was buzzing, and the last thing I wanted was to be by myself

In the early hours of 24 July 2006, the metal door on my pod clinked shut and I was well and truly alone in Iraq – I felt as far away as I had ever been from those nearest and dearest to me.

Dropping my bag onto a strangely familiar navy blue sofa and pacing about my new space, I broke my first rule of not smoking inside within about 20 seconds. With the air conditioning whacked up to full volume, the exploration of my new living space began. There was one small window, looking out onto the pod opposite and everything was painted landlord Magnolia. There was a compact shower in a diminutive bathroom, a tiny kitchen area with a microwave and a fridge – in the latter of which someone had very kindly left a can of drink and a fresh cheese sandwich. There was a kettle, cups and plates and some ropey, dried out tea bags and coffee sachets. A living area boasted a table, sofa and TV, and the small bedroom area contained a chest of drawers, cupboard and single bed. I grinned to myself, the whole place was kitted out in standard Foreign Office furnishings! The same as I had seen in Brussels and Bratislava, and now Basra. For some reason this made me laugh like a mad woman.

"Right," I said out loud, trying to get a grip, "time to get clean". And it was only when I had peeled off my filthy salty clothes (linen is a cool look for the desert apparently) and had a decent scrub under the rather delicious shower that I bothered to look in the mirror. What I saw took me aback: huge blue and black bruises spread across each shoulder which at first I didn't understand, but then realised that they were in the shape of my backpack, which had been heaved onto me, over the top of 12kg of crushing body armour, on and off for the past 36 hours. I poked the bruises but they looked worse than they felt. Longing to put on some clean clothes, I padded into the living area, leaving myself deliberately wet to get maximum benefit from the cooling breeze in the air-conditioned room. A crumpled sarong was fished out of my bag and wrapped tightly under my arms so that it would not drop when unpacking the rest of my kit onto the sofa. There was no way on earth I was going to get to sleep in a hurry and frankly, although it was already the early hours, the very thought of lying down and *relaxing* was perplexing in itself; unpacking seemed a preferable option.

Musing over the things that had been carefully chosen back in England to accompany me on my adventure (it seemed like a lifetime ago) - I remember thinking that the box of Lego reconstruction workers would make some hilarious photographs. In fact my laughter had made me ache all over as I picked them out of the box — a nurse, a teacher, a fire-fighter, even what looked like a little civil servant with glasses on a bicycle. "Everything Iraq needs!" I joked to my friends as they knowingly exchanged glances in silent agreement that I had clearly lost my mind. My visions were of setting up photo shoots with my fellow Lego friends in the desert sand, perhaps back-dropped by real troops or authentic Iraqis. Ashamed at the stupid idea, I stashed them into the bottom drawer and they would never see the light of day again. They are probably still there now. If the drawers are still there. If the pod even still exists.

Looking at the contents of my bag, anyone would have thought I was bound for retreat or a relaxing holiday — not the strange and violent world I would experience. Along with basic clothes (yet more linen) - all long sleeved, long skirted or combat-style trousers, I had bought colourful sarongs and scarves which I now draped around the place rather than hide them away in cupboards. Sketch pads, water colours and chalk pastels were unpacked. Lots of sun cream; my half written novel; green tea; my iPod and its dock; a Tai Chi book (along with written instructions for my ten minute form); Salam Pax's *Baghdad Blog;* Jack Kerouac's *On the Road* (which I love, but it never really chimed with me for this escapade); and photos of my friends and family. The photos were left face down for some time to come, I was somehow unable to bring myself to think about them in the context of this place.

47

Eventually, I think the adrenaline must have worn off and a wave of exhaustion knocked me into my bed at about six a.m. The phone woke me a few hours later, at around nine. It was Chris, who was coming to get me to show me around in half an hour.

The first day was of course filled with administrative jobs, although with a glimpse of my desk waiting for me, I was itching to get to work. I first needed to have a security pass made up (which is different from a made-up security pass), get an email account established, be issued with a laundry bag, and visit the small shop which sold confectionery, basic toiletries, alcohol, cheap fags (phew) and pot noodles. The latter confused me somewhat – as did the presence of a microwave in my kitchen, not to mention the sandwich from the previous night – because a terse note left in my pod reminded me that eating in pods was strictly forbidden - it encouraged rats apparently. It was to be the first of many confusing and sometimes amusing contradictions about the place. I would understand Joseph Heller like never before.

At a security brief I learnt about the Jaish Al Mahdi (aka the Mahdi Army or simply JAM) who were reasoned to be our number one night-time attacker. I wanted maps and pointing sticks, but got PowerPoint and nasty photos.

My introduction to the management section staff included delivery of the bloody batteries. They gave me advice on how to get through the dining system: 1) Leave body army on the floor and helmet in a pigeon hole outside the cook-house. 2) Wash hands properly – a note reminded us of vile diseases caused by lack of hand washing. 3) Take tray and queue akin to usual canteen behaviour. 4) After eating, return tray to kitchens. 5) Under no circumstances remove food from the kitchen. There it was again. What *was* the microwave for then? 5) Retrieve body armour/helmet and don't linger.

A tour of the compound revealed that I was living in a complicated warren of pods and Hesco walls. Hescos were huge, sand filled, wire meshed bags that when stacked together provided a wall of superficial protection.

Everything looked yellowy brown. And everywhere was blisteringly hot. Literally. Just to give you an idea 54°C is 10°C hotter than the hottest bath you would run for yourself and only 6°C cooler than a sauna.

Introductions were made to what seemed like hundreds of new colleagues. Hundreds of new *male* colleagues, that is. I was really not prepared for this. A quick flashback to the Foreign Office Fine Rooms.... a lunchtime briefing by the Iraq Policy Unit several months earlier as part of their recruitment push for Iraq. I stuck my hand up to catch the attention of Britain's Ambassador to Iraq, Mr Dominic Asquith: "Erm....Ambassador...I am going to Basra soon, and I can't help noticing in the film you just showed me that there aren't many...erm.... girls in Basra. What exactly *is* the male to female ratio there?"

He charmed me then, as he would at our every meeting, "About 50/50 amongst FCO staff," he flashed a smile and moved on to the next question.

I felt reassured by his response, but now in Basra, it dawned on me that actual FCO staff numbered only about 10 or 12 people, and whilst it was quite true that 6 of them were women, the remaining 360 people living on the FCO compound were in fact male. KBR (formerly Kellogg, Brown & Root a former Halliburton subsidiary) provided our life support – cleaning, laundry, food, etc and were 100% male; Police Advisors all looked very manly to me; Dog trainers = male; Perimeter guards were all fellas. And Control Risks Group (CRG), who provided our close protection and private security? Yep. All men. I felt duped, and said so to the (female) management assistant. She laughed in a make-the-most-of-it kind of way, and I laughed too, but inside a creeping acknowledgment of the need to have a careful think about this. The men on this camp were like none I had seen before. They were bristling private security men, burley prison governors, tough Ulster policemen – and even the Department for International Development (DFID) team looked like they could pack a punch. They shaved their heads, they worked out (to extremes) and the majority of them knew how to handle a weapon (no innuendo intended). The women I had met so far were friendly but brusque, almost sharp - clearly used to asserting themselves in a male environment. I didn't want to become like that. How to retain dignity, poise and ultimately, femininity, in a place like this? Thinking back to the contents of my backpack and the floaty silk scarves that decorated my pod, I felt like some shameful girly hippy. But determined to stay quintessentially *me*, I stalked off to the cook-house to talk to the chef about my vegetarianism.

Later that day, despite the Press Section laptop being mysteriously missing, I managed set up an email account and to get a message to my friends back home. *"So, I have arrived!"* I chirped as I recounted my journey and likened myself to Private Benjamin. Although I queried what a girl like me might be doing in a place like this, my tone was upbeat and mainly filled with the excitement of it all, in an attempt to reassure them that I was in fact quite safe. Which is far from what I felt. Those nasty Power Point slides stayed with me. Blimey. I could get injured, killed even. What had I done?

After writing the email and speaking to the family, who were excitedly on their way to my in-laws in South Africa, I ventured into the cook-house. The beaming smile of Saman, the Sri Lankan chef greeted me. He now knew not only of my vegetarian ways but of my time spent in his country and in my honour had specially prepared a veritable feast of vegetarian curried delicacies. Sitting down nervously at a table with my new FCO colleagues, the cook danced across with yet more delights. Thanking him in his native tongue, which pleased him further, I glimpsed a swell of Sri Lankans peering out at me from the kitchens. Giving them the thumbs up and tucking in, I was reminded of a time a few years earlier, on a tea estate in Nuwaraeliya, Sri Lanka. After serving up supper, the estate cook took it upon himself to stand at the table and watch closely until every mouthful had disappeared, like a patient parent feeding a toddler. Once finished he clapped his hands in pleasure and removed my empty plate. It was perhaps the most uncomfortable -

but tasty - meal I have ever had. I was glad that this wasn't going to be a repeat performance.

This food was good and hot - a decent Sri Lankan curry, not like the gentler Indian kind. My colleagues were not impressed. At first they offered a friendly jibe and a joke - that I had only been in theatre five minutes and I was already a favourite - but after about five days of the special treatment, an official complaint was lodged and I was called before the Management Officer. By this time I was thoroughly fed up with curry and longed for the regular bland vegetarian option – so the insistence that this practice needed to cease was welcome by me. Alarm bells were ringing however – and a certain insight was gained into the small-mindedness that festers in isolated compound communities. Same with the no food in rooms rule. Was this control by food?

So for the remainder of my time in Iraq, I would eat the perfectly adequate canteen food along with everyone else. Delighted and laughing off the slightly over-the-top official warning, I told Saman and the others that as delicious as their food was, to continue eating it was forbidden. The only consolation they had was in sneaking me out some *wadai* and even jaggery cake from time to time, once I got a bit braver about breaking the rules. I never did get egg hoppers though.

My first mortar attack (they say you remember your first and it's true)

During the day, when busy with work or in the cook-house, I was surrounded by people. The bar provided good company, and even for the short walks between the fortified buildings that made up our compound I fed on chatty banter with anyone and everyone; from the Iraqi laundry man and the one armed gardener; to exchanging a few newly learned Nepalese words with our perimeter guards. I got to know the Zimbabwean dog handlers and their dogs – Debbie the German Shepherd was a particular favourite. There were members of the Danish police who always enjoyed conversation; and I loved chatting to Taha, our one remaining Iraqi advisor. As friendly as this was, I know myself well enough to know that this constant desire for talking was largely driven by my fear of being alone.

On my first night in camp I had collapsed into slumber wearing just my sarong, yet it was weeks before I was relaxed enough to get undressed again for bed. True enough, I had managed to strip down to my swimming costume and take the occasional dip to take the steam out of the 54 degree heat, but at the pool I was not alone and therefore didn't feel as vulnerable (although in coming months I would find myself both alone and vulnerable there).

Once the day was over, and colleagues had been bid goodnight it was just me in a concrete bunker, all alone in Iraq. It was these quiet moments that were the hardest during my first few days at the Palace. My life at home was so full of friends, children and family that I rarely spent time on my own. And to be honest, even outside of Iraq I hadn't been entirely comfortable in my own company. So I faced all my demons at once – this was the extreme cold turkey approach to learning to be with yourself. My main fear was quite basically of being killed and leaving my children without a mother (I know, I know, I should have thought of that before volunteering). My second fear was (having been sternly told to acquaint myself with emergency evacuation procedures) that I would not be ready to get out in a hurry –

53

despite the obligatory emergency bag packed by the side of my bed. Back home, some young Sri Lankan friends had joked that their parents still had a suitcase packed on top of the wardrobe "just in case" even though they were safe in Tooting. I wondered if I would become like them? My emergency suitcase was a small maroon coloured holdall, and I would often wake actually clutching at the handle of the bag and nearly falling out of my bed. It was not unlike my fitful sleep some 12 years earlier on bringing my first baby home from hospital − so concerned that my little girl would stop breathing in her sleep that I would rest a gentle hand on her chest as she slept in the Moses basket next to my bed. There was less tenderness as I clutched my holdall of course!

As well as the maroon bag, I had a small pouch that carried my passport, a pocket torch, a list of phone numbers, photos of my family, a pen, a notebook and my fags. And yes, I slept with this around my neck too for the first week or so. The other dilemma was my boots. I actually wore sandals to work most days, but I knew in an emergency my sturdy desert boots were best, plus (allegedly) you weren't allowed on a military aircraft without proper ankle covering foot attire, said the rules. My boots were difficult to lace up at the best of times and would be impossible in a hurry, so the safest option seemed to be to sleep with them on my feet, loosely tied. As you can imagine, this was not conducive to a decent night's kip.

The air-conditioner also bothered me. With it on, the air was cool and dry but it almost completely masked any outside noise. Many times a night I would rush to switch it off because my ears tricked me into hearing "something" outside. And until I actually heard my first explosion in Iraq, I wasn't really sure what sound to expect. Would it be a crash? A kerr-boom? A thud? A crack? However with the air-conditioning switched off, although you could hear a pin drop, even in the dead of night, the heat meant that it wasn't very many minutes before I was a sweltering mess − especially fully dressed with my boots on.

I didn't have to wait too long before I witnessed my first IDF attack. IDF means indirect fire – but it felt pretty direct to me (or maybe it is "in direct fire"). I was outside and on my own at the time, which is a zillion times worse than being inside - it is flipping loud outside and the ground shakes.

I had been in the bar that evening, which was another reinforced concrete building. The ceilings were high, the lights were bright and lusty MTV videos were projected onto the wall as people played darts or pool or sat and chatted on more FCO furnishing. I met another man named Chris (there were four Chrises in total!) This Chris was an ex-RAF chef who worked for KBR and managed the team of Sri Lankan cooks as well as volunteering to work behind the bar. Like any good barman he was full of quips, but the first thing I noticed about him was that, unlike the others, he had his ID card strapped to his upper arm. I took the mickey and we were instant friends.

Chris and I - together with every other heavy smoker - spent most of our evenings huddled in the disabled toilet at the bar, which was the designated smoking room. There was no air conditioning and no ventilation in a room that was built to house just a toilet and a small table. Even with the door open, by the time five of us were in there it was so crowded we were virtually sitting on each other's laps and the air thick with smoke. We managed to get at least ten people in there one night, including the much tattooed Sid, who despite being from the military side of camp, wore nasty shiny 1970's shorts. I mention his shorts only because his testicles had the habit of squeezing themselves out of them whenever he sat down – so I usually chose to sit next-to rather than opposite him for fear of getting an eyeful of bollock! Apart from his tendency to inadvertently expose himself, he was a lovely guy.

Two things struck me about the smoking room - firstly, that it might have been less of a risk to our health if we actually smoked outside in the open air and secondly - who in their right minds thought a disabled toilet was necessary in a place like this? We had to fill in a million forms and pass a medical to get here, surely anyone disabled would have been considered an evacuation difficulty?

So on about day three of my time in Basra, I emerged choking out of the smoking room, donned my body armour and helmet and prepared myself for the 100 yard dash to my pod. The bar was usually only open for two hours an evening and it was near enough closing time. I had my torch at the ready and my door key in hand. I was in good spirits, despite having drunk next to nothing (being drunk in Iraq held little appeal). I swung open the heavy metal double doors and stepped out, embarking on my scuttle home.

After just a few steps, a huge explosion shook the ground; I froze. I could hear the faint pattering of shrapnel landing nearby. Then another occurred, not quite as close but still loud. What should I do? Throw myself to the floor? Run like buggery? Hug a Hesco? Another explosion, closer this time. I felt a hand on my shoulder and I felt myself being dragged back into the bar – one of the CRG security team guys had clocked me leaving and worked out that I would have been in the thick of it and bravely headed out to pull me back inside. There were nine mortars that landed in all (no one was hurt, miraculously). By the time the ninth one landed I was back inside the disabled toilet and my new smoky friends were laughing – "we thought you were going home!?" Then the sirens started up and the recorded voice over the Tannoys urged us to stay under hard-cover. No shit. Everyone groaned as the grills across the bar were pulled meaning the bar had closed and I faced the first tedium of lock-down until the security teams had made safe the main routes. We were stuck in the closed bar for what seemed like hours.

It was true that in the first few days I couldn't sleep through being so worried about leaving my children without a mother, but once I experienced that first attack and after witnessing a couple more quiet thuds in the dead of night, it was amazing how quickly one adjusted to the situation. They say you remember your first, and it was true, I wasn't ever quite as deeply frightened as that first time outside the bar – despite the increase in attacks and the loss of life to come. Sometimes the sirens would go off even before a missile impacted – somehow the military system could pick them up - although never to prevent or intercept I hasten to add. During the day as soon as we heard the noise of the alarms, we gathered into back corridors away from windows. Knowing which papers to grab to keep us busy, we also became adept at holding meetings in the shadows of our inner sanctum. We got to know each other quite well in this way - a bizarre form of team-building. When we were not under attack, the first floor of the British Embassy office building where we worked had a hushed, grey, museum feeling. It was a stale and creepy office, a little dirty and featureless, unlike the splendour of some of the buildings in the Basra Palace compound that lived up to the name rather better. Because of staff shortages and the mass exit of Iraqi staff we had no cleaners, so it was also dirty and dusty with overflowing bins. I wasn't surprised to learn that the room next to mine had been used as a makeshift morgue when the British army used the building at the beginning of the war. It was a cool and eerie room which I avoided. Philippa, who was Head of Chancery as well as being my manger, had her office in the former morgue. She had tried to set up a small meeting space in there using comfortable chairs – but none of us really used it. Goosebumps.

Keen to be surrounded by others, welcoming people into my office become important. There was no press and information section at all when I arrived, so I went about rearranging the office until I could offer a small reference library, pooling my own books and magazines and encouraging others to do the same. For the first time newspapers were provided (with the help of our Embassy in Kuwait). A hot desk was created for anyone who wanted to check their emails. But the sad fact was that people rarely graced my office - they just weren't passing by. Most of them were out and about meeting real Iraqis - training police or advising on agricultural projects; or simply because their security clearance did not allow them into my office building at all. It really wasn't the best place for an information point, all things considered. Eventually the newspapers were moved to a rack in the bar — a far more sensible idea. Until the bar stopped being used, that was.

My connection with the world and oddly, with my journalist friends in Basra, was via email. I would find myself glued to the screen for hours, hands dancing across the keyboard, researching online, where the cranky secure network would allow, and responding to a never ending barrage of queries from London and Baghdad. Only our military liaison officers in the room next to me stayed in their offices longer. They were making a point I think — they were military, they were hard and NO-ONE EVER worked longer hours than they did (I'm sure they were playing mine-sweeper half the time). It gave me great pleasure to call them lightweights and pussies at every opportunity and it amused me no end if I arrived first to open up the offices in the morning. It almost made up for their annoying insistence on calling me "ma'am". But I had to hand it to them; they did do a first class briefing EVERY morning in the High Commissioner's office. They used proper maps and pointy sticks and even grid references and sticky labels to describe the IDF and other attacks the British had come under in the previous 24 hours. When I first arrived I was VERY impressed; but after a few weeks once the ice had been broken between us, I began to tease them for their gallant efforts. Although different creatures perhaps stereotypically representing our organizations, we rubbed along pretty well, and when Mike, a Captain from the Territorials (a copper in real life) left Basra, he left me his desert combat uniform. His huge trousers were given away at a small birthday party for a friend after a very difficult week and they were last seen being worn over the legs of a slightly swaying American Diplomat. The shirt is used today as a painting smock and still very much treasured — a sentiment which often gets misconstrued.

It was often dark by the time I left the office in the evening and the main motivation to stop work by then was to eat. The cook-house was closed by eight (I should say 20:00hrs) and we all know that it was forbidden to eat in one's pod. Even with the sun gone it was still very warm outside and the difference between the outside heat and my air-conditioned ice-tomb of an office always took my breath away (as did the cigarette which was usually lit the moment I stepped outside). Shining a torch around never really made me feel comfortable. It was, after all, a war zone and remembering my grandparents' tales of blackouts during the war, flashing a light around went against the grain. But the desert night was black and the ground was rather uneven so I flicked a small credit card sized flashlight (that I kept in my body armour) on and off to guide the way. A few weeks later a female army officer friend, Olivia, taught me how to use my peripheral vision for seeing in the dark. Fond memories of her bounding around in front of me on the blackened compound shouting instructions for me not to look directly at the path. It works. Being outside at night was marginally more fun once that discovery had been made and the tiny skill made me feel ever-so-slightly less like a sissy civilian who was totally unprepared for life in a combat zone. Who was I kidding!?

The flashlight was still carried with me anyway, along with a trauma bandage, which I had been taught to apply but now dreaded being faced with a situation where testing it out became a reality. My radio was usually clipped into one of the pockets of my combat trousers, but because it was heavy and because over time I began to lose weight, if I travelled more than a short distance it would slowly pull my trousers down, if I wasn't careful. I also had to carry my pod key, my Iraqi mobile phone, phone lists, pen and paper (crucial as I never knew when a journalist would call), fags, a lighter, money (US dollars), my passport and various ID cards. This lot (together with my body armour and helmet) was supposed to go everywhere with me. I'll bet most reading this won't have ever used all the pockets on combat trousers!

A bizarre mental checklist was carried out every time I moved from one place to another, to ensure that everything was with me. Several times in fact, the mental check would be made. Sometimes three times. On return to my normal life back home in the village, I found that the whole checking-I-have-everything-before-I-go-anywhere thing was difficult to shake. I understood through my assessment for

Post Traumatic Stress Disorder (PTSD) when I got back to England that I was suffering something very common – hyper-vigilance.　Luckily it made me smile more than anything, sometimes we humans can be a little too adaptable and our new lives can be habit forming, but I was glad it wore off after a few months.　Forgetting front door keys/purse/phone these days isn't such an unusual occurrence.

Although carrying the body armour and helmet around everywhere wasn't fun, it was clear how life-saving it was. During my first few weeks in Iraq a young soldier was killed by mortar attack at another military base in town.　Rumours were flying around that he was inside a soft cover building and had allegedly died of shrapnel injuries to his head.　I was moved by the death of the young soldier, as I know my tight-lipped colleagues over at Media Operations at the Air Station were, when they called to give me the press lines for the tragedy.　Although the inquest showed the rumours were untrue, at the time we questioned whether we should be wearing out helmets indoors too.　We rarely did (although nearer the end it became increasingly common) but we often wondered just how strong our own so-called "hard cover" buildings were, especially our pods. This was something we would find out later.

Writing again to my friends in the English village of Bourn on 31 July, I light-heartedly skipped over danger.　An extract:

> *Dear Friends,*
>
> *I missed my self-imposed deadline of emailing you on a Thursday in time for any likely Thursday get togethers, but I guess you are all on summer recess and at various sunny locations around the world, so you will forgive me.*
>
> *I've been here over a week now and I am getting into a routine.　I have at last been able to sleep (despite the silly nonsense going on outside at night).　This I put down to a complete rearrangement of furniture in my pod.*

[I am not convinced that it was Feng Shui alone that was helping me sleep – more likely acclimatisation to danger].

Please understand that I won't be able to answer all of your questions for obvious security reasons (a great line which I intend to use with my work with the media).

In my first week I have hooked up with a girl called Nadia who was working here just a few weeks (now left) and we toured the shops available to us on the compound. We found four (but only two were open). I bought some postcards and for some reason an Iraqi football shirt that doesn't really fit me. Apart from her there is no (repeat no) girl friend potential out here. Most of the likely candidates are entrenched in the male dominated society (e.g. a "girls' night in" at my suggestion was almost laughed at). So I will have to make do with my own company for the most (which is cool - enjoying swimming, Tai Chi and artistic pursuits) and the occasional bit of male company (lots of hard core 40-something's who "ain't afraid of jack shit"). Saying that, everyone has been friendly and welcoming, but I sense an amount of gossip and bitchiness akin to the Big Brother household. I asked the medics where the diary room was, I don't think they got it.

[Note: the *"I will have to make do with my own company – which is cool"* line. It couldn't have been further from the truth!]

It's my day off today (though I have put in a half day). So I am in my pod with my iPod (a theme emerging here) thrashing out some reggae and drinking diet coke (I am a virtual T-total these days). May go to the bar later. With any luck they will get the Karaoke (spelling?) out again and I can treat the troops to my second mind-blowing rendition of the Fugees "Killing me Softly" (!)

61

Thanks for all your emails by the way - which are really keeping me sane.

I also replied to my friends individually in this weekly email. It wasn't a very personal approach – but I remember being under some delusion that I was making some sort of important 1940's war torn despatch by homing pigeon, and as rushed as it reads, much effort was put into these emails to sound as gung-ho and chipper as I could. I continued:

Janet, it's always good to hear about the English countryside and rain. And no, nothing could really prepare me for this place. And a second "no" - I am not putting in a transfer for South Lebanon (what a mess). Enjoy Greece and regards to your other half (had no idea he was such a wild fool!)

Clair - thanks for the offer of nail varnish. Not sure it will get through the Diplomatic Bag. I have pale pink and blue, and Nadia has left me her nail varnish remover, so I am off to a flying start. I am thoroughly fed up with my four changes of clothes already (hence the football shirt purchase). See above in answer to your questions on female population: "thin on the ground" is a fair conclusion. I hope to be in Kuwait for the start of the school term - and I am trying to secure a US black hawk for the trip - watch this space.

Till next week, my pals. God I miss you all.

Was I was some kind of Bridget Jones of Basra? Good god, they really had little idea of my predicament – and by the sounds of it, neither did I. Nail varnish? A girls' night in? Reggae and diet Coke? I ask you.

Actually it was very therapeutic writing to my friends back in England. It forced me to consider the lighter side of things and to stop seeing myself as some hard-core bitch on a mission to bring about world peace. Perhaps I should have continued writing to them forever more, as the tendency to take myself a little seriously still lurks. But the girls were my life-line to a welcome reality – a reality contained safely in a world of peace, deep in the English Countryside.

Writing again to my friends a week later the tone continued to be light-touch. This time the message chirped on about how the poor internet connection was effecting my online shopping - I was trying to buy my mum a birthday present - but it totally failed to mention how the lack of connectivity seriously hampered my operational effectiveness at work. Whilst the office was hooked up and networked, our pods would often drop out – it all depended on how many people were online and how close you lived to the main server. My military colleagues spat their tea when they learned that we had internet connections in our pods, but to be honest, especially working in press and media I felt the need to be connected to news and world events (and my email) at all times. Notwithstanding the number of occasions we were locked down in our rooms during or after rocket attacks and had no option but to work from there. I even set myself up a Basra Palace hotmail account so some level of work was achievable when access to the FCO system was impossible. Plus, as already explained, I wasn't in the habit of sleeping much, so it was good (if not always healthy) to have work to occupy some of those more lonely night time moments.

One thing that was reported to my friends back home (again in a very Bridget Jones fashion) was the discovery of Tash. Nadia, who accompanied me on that shopping trip and left me her nail varnish, was only in town for a couple of days and I was struggling once more for female company. The arrival of a female Major from the Territorial Army (with a previous military career) was very welcome. She had already done one official tour at least in Iraq, and knew many of the personalities at the base already - not least Mark Etherington, who she had shared some experiences with when he was Governor of Wasit Province during the CPA days (you will have to read his excellent book for that story!) Tash was blonde, slim and pretty but looked like she could pack a punch. She was confident, funny and highly organized and within a very short time it felt as if she had always been there and we had always been friends. She was also just beginning to fall in love with someone left behind in England (who she is now married to), so the timing for her wasn't brilliant, but it was good for the both of us to have someone to REALLY talk to about life, love and fear of IDF in those early days. Tash also introduced me to the jeep belonging to the Provincial Reconstruction Team (PRT), which we commandeered at the slightest excuse to get around the base. Tash used the jeep to collect mail from the army side and we sometimes had meetings on the American side of camp — the jeep saved us from a long hot walk. We didn't have much room to take the jeep for a spin, the whole base being only about a kilometre in length, but we tried to take silly detours so that we could truck over the dusty uninhabited UN terrain around the main Palace buildings — it was as close as we got to "getting out and about", but I remember laughing a lot and we churned up Iraqi soil in billows behind us.

Da Medja Massive and a *Better Basra*

Tash was not just good female company, she was a great help and very keen to get involved in my work – she could see I was severely stretched for resources. We didn't allow our visitors to have weapons on them when they came onto the FCO side of the base, and Tash helped me challenge and disarm the military escorts who arrived with visiting journalists. The jeep proved handy for taking the weapons to a safe lockable place on the military side. The situation felt totally bizarre – and tabloid headlines streamed through my brain..."Mum-Of-Three Disarms in Basra"...."Woman Runs Guns in Iraq"...."Civilian Softie Locks Up the Military".... Photo of British Diplomat with armfuls of automatic rifles – grinning like a buffoon.... "Diplomat is Fully Loaded". Being in the TA, I don't think Tash understood how completely out of the ordinary it was for me to be handling weapons, but she laughed along with (or possibly at) me.

The camaraderie and support was about to increase further. By the time Jason, the Arabic spokesman seconded from the FCO Press Office arrived, two weeks after me, the ground work for a functioning press and public affairs section had already been laid – but his help was still crucial. Key to Jason's role was establishing meaningful contact with the estranged Iraqi journalists; and the Consul General agreed. Perhaps the most difficult aspect of my work was my tasking to produce a "communications strategy" for HMG's efforts in Southern Iraq. I had no idea what one of these was, and suspected it would open a can of worms at a time when all I wanted to do was get on with the job - the task was a huge frustration. It baffled me that previous press officers had survived without even having a television in the building. I ordered one, it never came – I used to dash to my pod to switch on Sky News to catch breaking news. Staff at the compound didn't even get to see British or other newspapers, were not exposed to reference books, nor did they have easy access to key papers. One of my priorities was to get on with informing the people working on the base about how they were viewed by the outside world (over the walls and beyond) and how and why this was crucial to their success. It was my first real lesson in why perceptions count and I was immediately passionate about it. There were people working on the base that didn't know exactly what their colleagues were doing and how it fitted into the overall scheme of things. To be fair this was usually through exhaustion and lack of time.

Aside from me, the military and the US Embassy Office both had staff tasked with doing press work, but they rarely connected. Iraqi visitors would go through the unnerving and uncomfortable security checks to get onto the FCO compound and would go through the whole rigmarole again the following day when they visited the American compound – there was no coordination of effort. The 35-strong military Information and Media Operations team based at the Air Station seemed to me to be providing stories from the frontline to British tabloids that would inform the British public about the "war" (less the reconstruction) but serve to mainly boost army recruitment. There was no Basra-focussed media monitoring at all that was being disseminated to staff, let alone to the Consul General. Communications frankly was in a frightful state, it felt to me like everyone was beavering away with blindfolds on. But although I knew that writing a strategy was the absolute right thing to do – I was too busy rolling up my sleeves and fire fighting to take it on and the task was initially resented.

It was only when I was offered the services of a consultant to come and help write the strategy that my professional pride felt bruised. I never forgot my own resistance to the idea that an outsider would come to carry out what everyone senior around me was saying was a "crucial element of my work". The more that was discovered about their chosen man, the more I hated it. He had a Germanic name, would be paid a small fortune (by my standards), was former military (a Royal Marine for godsake) and would be there to solve the whole communications strategy dilemma within just two weeks. So in the weeks before he arrived I spent every spare minute of time - when I wasn't on the phone to journalists, reporting to London or trying to enlighten my colleagues - in my pod writing, what I thought was a first class communications strategy for HMG's efforts in Southern Iraq. Uncovering a number of other strategies from other places to use as templates (I even picked up one from Sierra Leone), I spent several lonely sessions exploring the notion of strategy in terms of communications and media. Brainstorming on your own isn't terribly productive! My first draft was presented to Jason when he arrived and it was clear to both of us that the can of worms had been well and truly opened. I am not one to do half a job.

In many ways it was worthwhile to have witnessed my own childish reluctance to accept outside help. From the moment Dieter arrived, every insecurity I felt melted away and he became part of the team instantly and he left Basra with a glowing report from me. In an ironic twist, a year later Dieter became my boss for a year, when, on a career break from the FCO, he helped me carve out a career as a communications strategist with a specialism in conflict. My unique insight into how narrow-minded government communicators can be is a real help to me today.

Hot on the heels of Dieter came David, a laid back Australian press officer from the Department for International Development (DFID). He was also there to help with the strategy and take a look at DFID's work in terms of communications. DFID had no resident press officer, neither did the British lead PRT – it was difficult to know where our work ended and it felt like I had the workload of ten men. One thing that was pretty clear was that having an "HMG" strategy for Basra might in itself give the wrong messages to our coalition partners. Lead by the General and the Consul General and backed enthusiastically by Tony Blair, the *Better Basra* plan was just beginning to take shape. Leaders of all the missions in Basra, including the Danish and the Americans and to some extent the UN, were beginning to gather at increasing regularity in the rather grand conference room on the first floor of the PRT building to discuss what would indeed make a *Better Basra*.

The British were driven by Blair's idea that *"we must commit ourselves to a complete renaissance of our strategy to defeat those that threaten us"*. Despite an impressive gathering of coalition partners around this, several of us pointed out that the important actors in this – the Iraqis - were missing.

I was tasked with presenting our communications strategy to this merry bunch, but felt quite strongly that the communications strategy should include the Danes and the Americans at least – and we would face potential disengagement from them if not. And so began a lengthy period of consultation which took up much of my 100 days in Basra. The text now required approval from Washington and Copenhagen and a complexity of British players and would face the inevitable compromises as a result.

In amongst all this I was experiencing my first bout of media visitors. Because a stop at the FCO compound always included an overnight stay, when I had visiting journalists in town they required 24/7 babysitting. The CNN crew sounded hollow laughs when our security manager told them they should move to hard-cover if we came under attack. "We are journos" snorted Michael Ware, a rough tough Australian reporter who had lived in Baghdad's red zone amidst bodies burning on the street, "when we hear an explosion we rush out with cameras". The BBC's Newsnight team were slightly more compliant, although – in defiance of the rules - camera woman Julie Ritson filmed as the helicopter landed at the base in the early hours of the morning – making them immediately unpopular. My guests were met by me and/or Jason at the helipad, and waved off by us when they left; we dined with them and accompanied them around the base. It was we who arranged people for them to interview, places for them to carry out the interview, and made sure they had clean accommodation, fresh sheets, functioning air conditioning, diets catered for, laundry done and room service (ok, not the last one).

Newsnight presenter Mark Urban managed some to-camera interviews in the pretty Palace gardens about our civilian work in Basra before I had to deliver them back to the military to cover "the war". Although delighted that they were getting more of a balanced picture, it always horrified me when journalists filmed in the gardens. As the rest of Basra suffered water shortages - despite the flowing Shatt-Al Arab waterway - our green grass and blooming foliage grated somewhat. Perceptions were bad — being housed in the Palace of a former oppressor wasn't a good move. A portrait of our Queen, which hung in our reception area didn't sit well with me at all. Time consuming and fraught with frustration, the visits of the Newsnight team, The Guardian, CNN and ABC news, were nevertheless all great practice for the arrival of the Radio 4 Today team, who were set to carry out live broadcasts over a number of days, and played a part in one of the most eventful weeks in my life.

Although there was no option but to continue with my "day job" as press officer, once I understood the nature of taking a strategic approach to my work (instead of being purely reactive), it felt odd operating in the absence of a strategy and writing this became my main preoccupation or "evening job". We comforted ourselves in the fact that we generally knew which direction we were going as media professionals: Trying to focus on the reconstruction efforts; the good things the British (and coalition in fact) were doing — which I have to say were many. We scrabbled around getting facts and figures on how many electric cables had been laid, how much of the marshes had been recovered for the marshland Arabs, and the success of the water treatment plant. We wanted to talk, not simply to the British media, but to International, Pan-Arab and local journalists — we had a hunch that they ALL mattered. Jason spent his life on the phone and even had friendly exchanges with the Iranian Al-Alam correspondents based in Basra - my eyebrows remained raised over that one.

Our Iraqi journalist contacts were beginning to tell us about how the Iranians were "influencing" what they produced. Several of them, although disillusioned with how the war was going, had suffered so badly under Saddam and lost so many in the war against Iran, felt that our efforts were their only hope. The fact that they risked their lives by even

69

talking to us was never taken for granted, and the bravery of the Iraqi who printed my press release on Margaret Beckett's visit to Basra word-for-word in his newspaper, won't be forgotten.

One of the toughest tasks in writing our strategy for communicating was to get the military on board. If this was clearly a strategy that represented the approach of the United Kingdom, we needed them to agree it. So an unlikely bunch consisting of myself, Jason, Dieter and David planned a weekend away at Basra Air Station to "engage with the military". I half wished we could have dragged Tash away from the PRT as she was a brilliant persuader – and had joined our "media massive". But the communications team consisted of me - a bolshie vegetarian diplomat that the Consul General had once called a "tree hugger"; an Aussie development expert complete with yellow T-Shirt and flip flops; a young Arabist and former journalist who had spent time in Yemen; and a former Royal Marine in designer clothes and suede shoes hardly fit for the desert (who we lovingly referred to as "the ponce"). If I had felt uneasy about the arrival of a solitary consultant, how would the top and medium level brass at the military headquarters receive the four of us? A more bizarre group of civilians in a war-zone you will never find.

The day before I arrived at the Air Station for my military meetings, a luxurious day's break from work provided an opportunity to write to my village friends. I had been in Iraq exactly a month.

> *25 August 2006*
> *Morning,*
>
> *I am actually taking a whole day off today. What the hell. I made the executive decision as I sat in a meeting at 11pm last night. There is work and there is work. As much as I lose sleep over how we can let the world know about the huge civilian reconstruction efforts we do in Southern Iraq, a girl needs sleep and a girl needs some space in order to function. Besides I*

am to board a helicopter tonight for a three day trip to Basra Air Station (our main military base in the south), work there will be 24/7. I need to engage with a few rogues who dwell under canvas. But I got what I wanted last night from the General (no not that – honestly). I noted in my book as he said in a meeting, "the military media operation hasn't taken the opportunities it could have done" (no shit General, but at least you said it and not me). I am armed with Arabic speaking Jason, a slick Media Consultant named Dieter, and also joining my media empire this week is David, the Press Officer from the Department of International Development.

Still find it hard to work out what day of the week it is. I spent Sunday stabbing out numbers on the phone, before I realised that my colleagues in Britain would be eating roast beef, walking their dogs and shopping in retail parks. Clearly worldwide there is a general lack of urgency to save the people of Basra – what's wrong with everyone?! (Just a bit obsessed at the moment....good plan to have the day off).

It clocked 54 degrees yesterday. Just a tad warm. Walking outside is like stepping into a pizza oven – so I rarely do it. My hair is like rats' tails as my head is constantly wet with sweat and tangled from the chlorine in the pool. Nice. Needing a bit of a makeover when I get to Kuwait in a few weeks. I have lost 4kg though and have a swimming costume tan (boy am I glad I opted for the boring black costume, often I am the only poolside female – you would think that was fun, but trust me, it gets tedious).

I speak to the family nearly every day and I am missing them, but I try to keep them firmly out of my mind for fear of cracking and becoming unprofessional. I was doing well until Alison sent me the "what does love mean" email. Usually I loathe chain emails of pictures of cute animals or lengthy unfunny jokes usually referring to gender, but this list

71

of sweet words out of the mouths of babes struck a nerve and I sobbed a little (ok, so clearly I WILL have issues when I leave here).

By the way ....I have checked with the Close Protection Team (first photo I sent you) for phone numbers, and they tell me they are a closely guarded secret. And the reason they are giggling is because they clearly didn't take my instruction to look like evil mean killing machines seriously enough. Can't get the staff.

Julia – At last. Saddam's Palace could do with a lick of paint, when you have finished on the house. Not sure about the pooh-green colour you describe though. Don't knock your own organisational skills – I have always admired them. Fancy a job in Basra? If you can organise a multi party family picnic to Wickstead, you are well qualified to help the Basra Provincial Council on their feet (piss up in a brewery analogy here). I tell you, forget India, the Canaries, and South Africa – Basra needs you! In fact if we withdrew all our troops and replaced them with middle aged house-wives we would soon sort the place. I can see us now with black bin liners and marigolds "clearing up the streets" and banging militias heads together ("he is not a militia, he is a very naughty boy"). Forget military imposed curfews – to bed with no supper would work (especially during Ramadan).

So I am off to read by the pool, at least until my phone rings and I have to explain our troop repositioning in Maysan to some BBC journalist.

Did you get the postcard sent to Bourn HQ by the way? Keep up the correspondence.

All my love as always
xxxxxx

The luxury of being able to email from my pod and have access to a swimming pool became all too clear once at the Air Station. Unlike Dieter, Jason and David, I managed to secure Red Sea freight container accommodation all to myself at the Air Station - one advantage of being female. A feeble air conditioner clattered into action taking the edge off the roasting heat and the faint smell of sweat emanated from the inappropriate nylon sheets. I shook my head in disbelief at my decision to bring a sleeping bag to Iraq with me. Having been told to pinch the backs of my hands to check for dehydration, I knew that uncurling this bag and climbing inside would see me on a saline drip within minutes. It did however, make a good (if rather slippery) pillow. A room of my own with a lock on the inside meant a good night's sleep and although I was not technically under "hard cover" (something that would bother me on later trips to the Air Station) – I knew the Air Station received far fewer incoming attacks and was built over a far larger area. Put bluntly – the odds of being hit and being killed were less. Plus, being surrounded by thousands of troops offered some notion of safety and I slept like a baby the first night there.

Periods were not something that were welcomed by me in Iraq, as we were rather emphatically told by the management team at Basra Palace that we were not to flush tampons down the toilet. We were given clear plastic bags to dispose of our rubbish in. I am very discreet about bodily functions and I felt so uncomfortable with the whole menstruating business that I considered taking the pill the whole time I was there (now...I know what you are thinking, don't jump to conclusions). So when I awoke on Britain's biggest military base in Iraq to find that although my bag contained a whistle, compass, list of Arabic phrases and a water bottle, I had no tampons with me and my period had started – I was less than pleased. *And* I had decided to wear white as I thought it might be cooler for our hikes across the desert base. It was early on a Sunday morning and I sneaked out of the scruffy Foreign Office compound area in search of a shop, which was quickly found: but it was closed.

My search for a female of child-bearing age was rewarded when a young girl soldier was spotted ambling amongst tents. The woman appeared not much older than my own daughter and tossed me a whole box of Lilets in a very matter of fact way. I felt like a fool and thanked her perhaps disproportionately and managed to conceal the situation to my three male colleagues whose only query was why I was eating Paracetamol and three bars of chocolate for breakfast. They didn't notice my white trousers fluttering dry in the sunshine outside my room.

By now my colleagues has started calling me "The Baroness", perhaps because I had started calling Jason "Ambassador" on account of an email I had intercepted from an Iraqi journalist in which he had addressed Jason as such – and notably Jason had not corrected the inaccurate assumption! Perhaps it was due to my modest dress, my strings of pearls, or my affable but snooty approach that the Baroness nickname caught on with military colleagues too. Or perhaps it was because in this hierarchy-based society I secretly quite liked the name. Anyway, there was utterly no way that The Baroness was going to share the fact that she was menstruating and had stomach and back cramps.

We continued on our mission and through the discomfort I managed to get through an incredible couple of days at the Air Station receiving brief after brief after brief from military colleagues. We learnt about media operations and psychological operations and information operations. We observed the fast-talking Charlie barking sound bites down the line to Britain's best selling papers. We met the polling team – who gathered public opinion data. And we looked at crude posters that were designed to deter Iraqis from planting roadside bombs (I have to say we shared our cynicism on the chances of success of the latter). Thank goodness we had Dieter with us. He was fluent in military speak and once he revealed he was a former "bootneck" this code seemed to relax whoever we were with. It enabled a ride in a snatch Land Rover to the cook-house and it meant that some of the media reporting and monitoring would at last be shared with their civilian colleagues. All this despite his poncey suede shoes.

As for the strategy however – Charlie and his fast-moving media machine were not terribly concerned with it. I began to understand the crow-bar separation the military applies between media and information work – to the FCO it is all about communications (but perhaps we have similarly confusing separation between communications and diplomacy). The media team were almost entirely re-active, responding to events, and took a dim view of their posturing, scheming, psychological operations side, which they viewed as bordering on propaganda and not as clean. I also understood the difficulties of asking for individuals in a tasking-based organisation to think creatively about strategy. The right entry level needed to be found to succeed – and I wasn't sure that getting buy-in from the General as part of the *Better Basra* plan was the whole answer.

A Female Olympian and the Two-Can Rule

We returned to Basra Palace in much the same fashion as before – a shuttle Merlin in the dead of night. Same hot night-time hustle. Same dilemma - do I watch the awesome flying beast arriving and risk bullet-like clouds of dust blinding me? Or should my back be turned to avoid retinal damage like a seasoned pro? The answer was somewhere between the two – with the help of some loaned eye protection. Military officers are ever chivalrous. I certainly got the most from those flights and began to love the whole process of getting in and out of the Palace. It never really occurred to me how precarious it was that I lived and worked in a place that was only considered safe to access at night by helicopter.

Jason and I didn't realise it at the time – but our short jaunt to the Air Station would be our only substantive time outside of the Palace grounds in our whole time together in Iraq.

The work continued and our commitment to it increased. The attacks got more intense and more often, but our resilience also grew, despite the challenges. We even began to enjoy ourselves and found bizarre ways to be entertained (beyond being holed up in pods watching endless DVDs which seemed to keep many of our colleagues amused). I was happy to report in my emails back home that the social scene had taken an upward turn. On one afternoon (when we hadn't had IDF to confine us indoors) we held "The Basra Olympics". A very improvised range of games at the barely used bar next to the lake, put together (literally) by the CRG security team. Being a bunch of body building hard men, their team won every round - with the sole aim of whooping the team from the US State Department. Our team, *The Basra Bobsleigh Team*, came a sorry last. But not before I completely embarrassed myself in a "I'm a Civil Servant Get Me Out of Here" special. We were to race 100 yards and down a can of beer as fast as we could, whereupon I spectacularly puked (it is all on film apparently). One bootneck quipped that I would make it into the Paras yet. Ha ha.

We may have come last in this challenge, but one thing us diplomats weren't half bad at was throwing a party. After making a tit of myself at the Olympics there was not much to lose, so the Consul General's assistant and I had a great laugh together abusing the compound-wide security Tannoy. Robin Lamb, the temporary Consul-General, had come to the end of his tour and it was his last night in town. Robin was a very popular man and staff were saying a goodbye to him in the PRT building. To announce his departure I made a loud Big Brother style announcement asking housemates to convene for the eviction. Robin's assistant chickened out despite her marvellous Geordie accent which would have been perfect. Howls of laughter echoed across camp — for once the Tannoys were bringing something more light-hearted than a bomb warning.

We then donned fine clothes and enjoyed a modest amount of fine wine at the farewell party for Robin. The military appeared impressed at the quick turn around from sports clothes and the five or so women amongst us scrubbed up exceptionally fine - some even had little black numbers and stilettos with them! Still feeling slightly unwell from the beer race I sulked in the corner with my usual long sleeved, long trousered "practical" clothes and a bindi on my head to mark the occasion. I had painted a postcard size picture of the Shatt-Al-Arab waters that flowed past Robin's office window and scribbled something on the back for him about wanting him to remember the beautiful side of a *Better Basra* — but I felt a bit of an unsophisticated fool somehow when it was presented to him.

Despite feeling underdressed and a bit of an idiot, the evening was relaxed and, for many of us, as close to usual diplomatic life as we could manage, despite a distinct lack of Ferrero Roché. (This is meant sarcastically of course).

Quietly going about their business, the Nepalese guards continued their smiling routines of perimeter security. They played volleyball during their time off — but what I didn't know was that they were preparing for the party of the year, and in true Nepalese fashion they killed a goat for the occasion. They bought one in specially, only they put it in the pen with the maintenance manager's pet "rescue" goats and got theirs mixed up with his favourite goat called "Dude". I left it to a meat eater to break the news to the maintenance manager when he got back from his R&R to tell him that they had all eaten Dude at a Nepalese party. He took it well (99 Ghurkhas can't be wrong).

I have to say it was the most peculiar yet enjoyable celebration I have been to. It was the festival of Dasain and shift B of the Ghurkha guards invited a handful of us to attend. I prised myself away from my desk and along with young Chris, the 22 year old clerk, we attended in representation of the Embassy office. We immediately became guests of honour and were forced to dance in the centre of about 30 delightful (and in no way leery) Nepalese men. I wish someone had taken photographs because Chris is well over six foot (and skinny with it) and I felt like the world's biggest female, swaying about in my shalwar kamiz next to the guards who must average about five foot tall. (NB - In no way take their height as an indication of their strength or ability). After several hours (yes hours) of Nepalese dancing and hand clapping, I realised that the only fault with these incredible people is their lack of tolerance for alcohol. Sweaty and still with my bindi on, they left me and Chris in the bar and by seven thirty, the place had transformed from Nepalese festival into a regular bar evening. Chris and I felt as if we had been in a dream, and our jaws were aching from grinning so much.

On the occasion of Chris's farewell a few weeks later, the "two can rule" had been firmly asserted - a daily recommended alcohol limit for us, enforced by the management team. Drink more and we received a stern warning. Do it again and we could be thrown off camp. Morale was dropping so we decided on a fancy dress theme to cheer everyone up. Chris was one of the most popular, helpful and smiley people on camp and a big crowd turned out to say goodbye. Everyone made do, making costumes from table cloths and anything we could find. Olivia came as

Zorro, young Chris as a hippy, and there were a number of super-hero costumes.

I pushed my own boundaries that night too. I had visited the American shop and stocked up on white-trashy clothes to come to the party as an "American". Big hooped earrings, denim shorts, tan tights, sneakers, US army T shirt and a baseball hat with an eagle and Iraq (pronounced *"eye-wrack"*) written on it. Thinking I was a real smarty-pants I even invented a fake US ID in the name of Missy Eagle – which to my horror gained me access to the American base a few weeks later. Spirits were high, despite our alcohol ban, and the new gum chewing me was barely recognised by my co-workers. I even got a few nods of approval from American colleagues, oblivious that the piss was being firmly taken.

You can imagine how horrified I was that night when my duty phone rang just as the party was hotting up at about 10pm. I was needed immediately at the helipad to meet an incoming CNN crew! I had no time to get changed. I only hoped that the body armour would cover up the worst offences – but body armour didn't really work with fake tan nylons and hot pants. You can imagine how my colleagues roared with laughter at my predicament. Perhaps the only time I had bared my legs ever on camp. What was I saying about perceptions being important?

The hooped earrings were still being prized out of my lobes when I greeted the team, and to my dismay, I realised that they were accompanied by Guardian journalist, Ghaith Abdul-Ahad. I quickly showed them to their rooms, however CNN's Michael Ware was particularly adamant that they needed a drink and kept asking if the bar was open. I explained the two-can rule (but had left some tinnies in their room) and that the bar was about to close, which was kind-of-almost true. What was really going through my mind was what happens when a hard-nosed Guardian journalist meets more British Diplomats dressed even more absurdly than I? A charge that we were not taking our mission in Iraq seriously could be graphically illustrated.

So a merry dance akin to Fawlty Towers ensued as I coaxed a battle hardy bunch of journalists into their pod, reminding them to "stay under hard cover!" should any missiles start landing. I think I already explained their response to this - they snorted their derision. Ware looked at my stupid denim shorts and asked me directly whether I was going to the bar. Lying to his face, he was bid a sharp good-night. Pausing very briefly in my room to change out of my ridiculous outfit, I did in fact head for the bar, cursing the two-can rule under my breath.

His last night in camp, Chris had somehow got around the said rule and the six foot hippy staggered out of the bar followed by a handful of very loud and slightly concerned friends. The helicopters were running very early that night and somehow Chris needed to be ready to embark in 15 minutes.

Clearly the threat of being sent home if found drunk didn't matter less to Chris, who was grinning lovably as he fell into the rose bed en route to his room. We dragged him to his feet. He still had flowers in his hair. And it was like this that Ghaith and Michael found us. They had stepped out of their pod for a cigarette and followed the noise of laughter. On introduction to the journalists Chris seemed to sober up enough to stand.

Michael merely looked at me and said, "you've changed".

Chris was taken back to his room, given an icy shower, slapped a few times no doubt and sent on his way to the helipad – which he successfully managed to climb aboard. I was next to see him in England – sharp suited and proper.

Leading the journalists back to their pod, sharing a smoke, the fancy dress party was explained. I came clean. I had wanted to keep them away from it, lest they got the wrong impression. It justified why I had looked like an overweight aerobics instructor and why Chris was sporting a large peace sign. I even told them about Zorro. We all laughed. But I was still very pleased that there was no photographic evidence of it all.

In a Man's World

Parties were rare, and although there was a sense of farcical humour to many of my experiences, the pressure was mounting. The good bits were the weight-loss, having time to paint and an alarming amount of "me" time, but being one of only a handful of women on camp took its toll.

Not all of the attention I received for being a female was welcome, and after only a couple of weeks there was a realisation that I needed to curb the invitations that were dished out when the bar closed in the evening. I had been welcoming handfuls of friends (men and women) back to my room to watch movies or hang out.

This sadly provided an opportunity for one chancer, whose intentions became all too clear when he found himself alone in my room at the end of one night. Everyone else had already yawned their goodbyes and left, I was tired and also in need of sleep. He didn't seem to take the hint, and as I got up to bid him farewell he slammed me against the wall, grabbed my breasts, and - rather revoltingly - actually sucked my neck. All the time this was happening (which, when now replayed in my mind seemed to last hours, but in reality can't have been more than a few seconds), I was internally kicking myself. I had been very green – my need for company was driven by a fear of being alone, not by a desire to sleep around and I knew then I had not made myself adequately clear. But although the man was a little tipsy, he was no rapist. I think I actually said "yeeeuuchch!" out loud as I peeled him off me (he was quite strong) and he blinked at me in confusion. Leaving through my own open door at top speed, minus the required body armour, I disappeared into the night.

Solace was found in the operations room and the burly security team who manned the decks round the clock poured warm tea for me. To be honest they were more distraught about the situation than I was. I am pleased to this day that the identity of my over amorous admirer was kept a secret, for I fear that those programmed to offer me close protection may have exceeded their brief that night. I had recovered myself to a state of nervous laughter, but some members of the security team were bent on defending my honour for some time to come. My protectors did not even seem content when I advised them that I had spoken to the gentleman concerned in the cold light of day and graciously accepted his stammering but heart-felt apology. The whole episode made me realise that I would have to toughen up even more and cope with spending time in my room on my own.

A few days after this event I was confused to be called to the front of the Palace Building by the head of the CRG security team and asked to bring my camera. Expecting some kind of serious security incident, instead I was faced with a bizarre scene. Every single member of the CRG team sat perched in lines on the sandy entrance steps to the office building. Assembled together, their biceps bursting from their polo shirts and grade one haircuts – they looked like the cover picture of a gay magazine. Of course I didn't tell them that! Parked in front of them was a forklift truck holding a wooden pallet. They cheered when I arrived and it was a while before it dawned on me that they wanted a group photograph and that, as "press-girl", I was the chosen photographer. Their sniggers were down to the fact that they expected me to climb onto the pallet whilst they hoisted me high in the air using the forklift to get a good aerial shot. I had to hand it to them – it was a brilliant idea and the pictures came out well – but I had to quash my fear of heights in an instant and tuck my skirts under my thighs to avoid sharing a glimpse of my underwear to the muscle below. I still smile to myself on thinking about it, and know that my absurd predicament contributed to their grins in the picture.

I was recently asked by a new friend whether being a civilian woman in such a testosterone-fuelled, military environment was a problem. I think being a civilian was far more of a problem than being a woman. Some civilian men really did not grasp their place in the scheme of things, and it appeared as if their masculinity was challenged by the presence and activity of the uniformed military, who were tearing in and out of the compound in tanks and seeing "real action". In a tense moment it was perfectly OK for me to turn to a soldier and say I was afraid, whereas civilian men may have felt obliged to display their bravery more. The military personnel I encountered appeared genuinely well trained to accept equal or higher-ranking women and it was encouraging that I seemed to be able to have a fairly frank and relaxed conversation with General Shirreff and other high ranking military officers. Maybe this was because of my role and the fact that I stood out as a civilian, but perhaps my gender difference allowed me to be more direct and communicate at a more human and compassionate level with the senior military than some male colleagues were able to.

I was also more likely to be met with sexual flirtation or with animosity by my civilian male colleagues, as opposed to my military ones. And gender played a part in some of the bullying that occurred as an inevitable consequence of living in a small community in difficult circumstances. One protection mechanism I used with tenacious and hostile alpha males was the fact that I was a mother - and for a while the only mother there. I reminded some on the base of their own mothers and was told so on more than one occasion. One member of the security team even called me "mum" despite being only a few years my junior and I found myself lending an ear to colleagues who had concerns about their relationships back home, not just with their wives, but with their teenage children and elderly parents. Being a mother was also a huge advantage when talking to Iraqis. I would find any excuse to bring my children into conversation and ask about their own experience as parents - you would see their eyes soften - sometimes in sadness - but usually in tenderness when they spoke of their families. We would compare ages and speak of the merits of having a girl as the eldest — mine was responsible and compassionate and helped her father with her little brothers in my absence. Some Iraqis spoke proudly to me about how educated their wives were and we were able to have real, meaningful dialogue about Iraqi women.

However, none of the journalists encountered were women, although I did spend time with a female judge. Unfortunately, as the judge spoke no English and my Arabic was poor, there was little bonding to be had but we smiled a lot at each other. Our relationship was helped along by a very brave Iraqi man called Assaf. Assaf worked closely with the female judge, spoke excellent English and often facilitated meetings between the PRT Justice, police and prison advisors and Iraqis. Working with a female judge had caused him problems, but he was as committed to a "better Basra" as anyone I came across in Iraq.

I mention the advantages of being a woman in a male dominated setting, because there is an assumption that men cope better in hostile and difficult environments, but perhaps there is a real case for acknowledging that some feminine qualities are crucial in such testing circumstances.

Despite the poor press that Islam sometimes gets, having lived in Islamic countries, it's clear that being a female can offer you some instant respect and protection within a Muslim environment. As Tony Blair said in his Foreign Policy speech at Reuters Headquarters, London in March 2006, *"To me, the most remarkable thing about the Qur'an is how progressive it is....it is inclusive. It extols science and knowledge and abhors superstition. It is practical and far ahead of its time in attitudes toward marriage, women, and governance"*.

Presenting myself as a friendly mother and ensuring my dress, body language or speech was never flirtatious has always ensued a gentle acceptance of me as an outsider. For some Iraqis the image of a British woman was one of promiscuity and low morals and, to be honest, picking up Britain's most popular newspaper or being in any small town centre in Britain on a Saturday night would support this perception - so I was at pains to dispel this myth and offer a face of respectability and professionalism. Hot pants aside of course; not getting too pious here.

Once or twice my Iraqi friends asked why I was in Basra and not with my children. Perhaps not being entirely honest with myself, I would tell them that my time in Iraq was short, but that Britain owed it to Basra to help improve life for its people. The breakdown of my marriage the moment I arrived home was perhaps more indicative of the real reasons for me being in Iraq, but in denial, at the time, my message to the people of Basra was that I was there because *I cared*. I knew that my male colleagues would not be asked questions on the same level.

Not to say that the men I worked with didn't care. I met many capable and compassionate men in Iraq: A prison officer who smuggled kittens into his room to avoid the routine cat extermination; a medic with a wonderful eye for photography who captured the faces of Iraqi staff on film with such sensitivity; and a Surrey policeman who was famous for his heartfelt line "I just love Iraqis".

One Friday evening I was working late when a soldier rather nervously came into my office. He had spent the day painting a school in downtown Basra, and was clearly tired and a little distraught. Re-decorating the school was part of an operation under the *Better Basra* scheme. It was basic reconstruction and hearts-and-minds stuff, but this soldier had some concerns. He told me that having spent a couple of days at the school, he was getting to know some of the children a bit – he spoke with genuine fondness for them. He described his duties and summarised by saying he thought fresh paint wasn't really what they needed. He had met a girl with a hole in her heart. Without an operation she would perish, but she was unable to get proper medical attention in Iraq. The solution lay with treatment in nearby Jordan or perhaps Kuwait. This, sadly, was not an unusual story. Touched by the child's plight, the soldier wanted to help, but his main frustration was that, even if he dug in his own pockets, the cash would be rejected because it was British money, and in taking the money the girl's family could become targets for militants opposed to our presence in Iraq. He had even gone as far as speaking to the girl's father, who had confirmed this. He told me all this in almost a whisper, "I was told you might be someone that could help".

With a heavy heart I knew I couldn't and didn't help the girl, but I hope in some way I helped the soldier by allowing him to express his sentiment – we talked for quite some time. I never saw him again, but I did meet many Brits – both military and civilian - who were quietly spending at least some of their salaries paying for Iraqis to educate themselves, or get medical treatment, or rebuild their lives. So distraught was I when I left Iraq I decided to forgo Christmas, instead giving every penny I had saved to Iraq's war widows.

Compared to the life of a woman in *real* Iraq my troubles were miniscule and although I had been widowed myself at a very young age, this had not meant I was socially outcast, unable to earn a living or support my family, like Iraqi widows. When I assessed how much danger I was in, I invariably compared my current situation to those on the other side of the wall, not with those safe back home in the village. I felt privileged.

But dangers did lurk of course, and the daily barrage of rockets and mortars were only part of the discomfort of living in Basra. Basra was more than twice as hot as Britain (an average summer high in London being 21°C, Basra temperatures frequently rose to above 50°C). Within days of arriving rehydration salts became part of my diet, as the medics said I was lacking in fluids. I battled with the quantities of water we were recommended to imbibe throughout my stay and frequently felt parched.

I paid another visit to the medics after I rather shamefully bumped my head during enthusiastic backstrokes in the swimming pool. Despite the medic's recommendation, I was far too embarrassed to get my lump checked out at Shiabah Field Hospital, especially given the reports in the UK press at the time that the FCO staff languished in luxury alongside suffering squaddies. Some of which was true –

although hoards of dirty troops could frequently be heard splashing around in the diplomatic pool!

I was almost pleased when, as a result of throwing myself to the ground, scuffs on my knees emerged and the bruises from carrying heavy kit for long hours reappeared. Not exactly war wounds, but a better mark of my experience than my silly swimming pool injury!

Most of the damage was psychological. The obvious security threat (literally) hanging over us played its part – but it was more the way it was handled by people rather than the danger itself that caused problems. Some colleagues took hyper-vigilance to extremes, became aggressive and nervous, sometimes irrational, but perhaps most soul destroying was seeing petty, but divisive arguments begin to brew in camp. The announcement of the two-can rule upset many who felt they were being babied by compound management. Some Danish friends rebelled and flaunted their habit of sundown gin and tonics. Others took to their rooms to drink (a backfiring of the new regime, I'd say) – and once I realised that the small shop on the compound was actually monitoring and reporting my alcohol purchases, even though it was usually bought for a group of us to share, even I felt a drop in my desire to obey the rules. I wasn't a big drinker to begin with but the two-can rule made me want to start! The management and security team had their hands tied behind their backs, their job was to keep people alive and working (in every sense) and with rockets and mortars landing inside the compound on a now daily basis – beginning to tear holes into buildings – it was only a matter of time before we had holes torn out of us. Drunk we must not be. But sadly, the reality was that the bar – perhaps the only real opportunity to relax in a day - soon became empty.

Loss and coping

I did actually break the two can rule – by drinking four cans of Fosters in one day about a month after I arrived.

One of my main concerns before leaving England was that my great-aunt would still be alive when I returned. She was in her eighties, but not completely frail, so I figured she would last my six month assignment. Whilst living in Sri Lanka my grandfather had passed away and although I made it back for the funeral at the time I regretted not being there for my mother and grandmother.

But not long into my time in Iraq, news came through from my mother that dear old Auntie Noreen had died. The end seemed peaceful, but I was wracked with guilt for not being there again for my mum and grandma (it was her sister) – and with the time it took to get out of a military theatre it didn't look like I would be able to make the funeral. I felt wretched, and was in need of support from my husband – support which he really didn't understand nor did he feel able to provide. I had barely shared with him the realities of living in Iraq, perhaps to spare him the worry, but perhaps because the cracks had already begun to appear in our relationship and I felt simply unwilling to share my new adventure. I wrote in my diary, *"being alone here has really kicked in and I have had a good old sob. I have spoken to my mum, but I really wish I could be in England to offer the family some support. Very bad timing Auntie Noreen, bad timing indeed".*

I coped with it all by locking myself in my pod for 24 hours, and only accepting select guests and certainly no neck suckers.

The four cans of Fosters hit my teetotal brain fast and emerging from my pod I headed for the bar only to slump into a sofa and blither on about communications strategies to some posh bloke in uniform. I found out at an obscenely early morning meeting the following day (another *Better Basra* soirée with the General) that the "bloke in uniform" was the Chief of Staff. My military liaison officer was horrified at my lack of deference in dealing with such a high ranking man. But Chief of Staff seemed to enjoy our meeting in the bar and needless to say I was far more articulate on the subject at the morning meeting, so he got my gist and I hadn't blown it.

Sharing my feelings about my aunt's death with my friends back home was difficult, again there was a fear that they would think me selfish for being where I was. I needn't have worried; their emails in return were always supportive and included just the amount of back home trivia needed to keep me strong. In one reply to their messages I wrote, *"loved getting your emails. Believe it or not it is very important to me that Pete has won Big Brother. Restores my faith in humanity, etc. etc. Fleur - Totally wicked to get your messages, they made me roll with laughter. I love you too, bird. You are right about the stilettos – what was I thinking coming to Iraq without them? But let me set the record straight – there was no tax payers' money involved in the beer drinking – I pay for every last drop. $2 a can if you must know – and on our new rules I can survive on less than $5 a day. You got me thinking though - if the Soviets can start up tours around Stalin's prisons, there could be scope for a forward thinking property developing girl to turn Basra Palace into a luxury spa..."*

You might laugh, but I still think to this day the Palace and grounds could be usefully transformed into a health resort – the flowing waters of the Shatt-Al-Arab breathing life into tourists and locals alike. Basra used to be the Venice of the Middle-East, I'd love to see it return to that. But it was far from a resort when we were there – some likened it to prison, but with Abu Ghraib in the headlines this felt like a tasteless comparison. The two-can rule was bad, but it wasn't torture.

As a coping strategy for my loss and recognising that we needed SOMETHING else to stretch our minds apart from work, Jason and I tried to take long, early evening walks around the compound as often as we could, once the heat of the day had lessened. Sometimes just the two of us would go; at other times we persuaded others to join us on our miniature adventures. Surrounded by ten foot high concrete T-walls our main ambition was usually to try and take in a view – to witness life beyond the fortress that we were living in. So our walks were usually peppered with climbs. We clambered rickety ladders inside look out towers called Sangers, guided by our Nepalese perimeter guards and we peered into Basra city through netted slits. We saw littered streets and quiet houses, sometimes people sitting talking, and occasionally children playing. I'll never forget watching a group of about six youngsters scampering on a flat roof top. They were giggling and chasing each other, hiding behind dripping, droning air conditioning extractors. They were pointing toy guns at one another and pretending to shoot. Was it cops and robbers or Brits and militias they played? I had a mixture of feelings sweep over me watching these kids – about the same age as my own – acting out a childish war in the beautiful dusk light. I wanted to reach out. I wanted their lives to be free of violence. But overwhelmingly I missed my own children.

One of our climbs took us high onto the top of the instantly recognizable Saddam's Gate (at the entrance to the Palace) – but we didn't linger for long – a sniper would have thought all his wishes came true at once to see the Namibian head of the perimeter guards, a head of DFID projects and three diplomats standing at one of the highest and most obvious places in town. It *was* high and I didn't make it to the last leg, instead took photos of the view and of my colleague's ascent. We also clambered onto the top of the PRT building and looked over the Shatt Al-Arab waterway into Iran across what was left of date palm plantations. Saddam had stripped Basra of their famous palms during the Iran-Iraq wars for fear the trees hid Iranian infiltrators.

The land across the waters still provided refuge to guys with guns. If the Iraqi journalists had got it right the militias that attacked us from there were also Iranian. On one of our walks around the compound, our small group was warned by a Nepalese guard that snipers could be seen aiming at us from across the river. Our ears played tricks on us and a multitude of sounds were heard and interpreted as the tap-tapping of gun fire. Remembering our hostile territories course we thought we knew that zig-zag running was the best method of running away from someone who has you in their gun sights. Preparing ourselves for a short zig-zagged sprint someone wisely pointed out that the tactic would be useless if our attacker was approaching us side on. We paused to consider our predicament. We had a 20 yard stretch to cover between us. Our solution, to the hilarity of the Nepalese guard, was to zig zag in the air – and we escaped the situation with a bizarre series of jumps and leaps. No one was hurt - perhaps because our assassin was all in the mind of a bored perimeter guard. But we laughed very hard at our ridiculous ingenuity.

Once we discovered the wreck of Uday Hussein's main Palace at the far end of the deserted UN side of the compound, we made exploring this our regular excursion. We usually walked, but Uday's place was so far it generally required the commandeering of a golf cart. Whenever I had a media visitor in town I would ensure they got to see these views and could often be found clambering back stairs of buildings with a camera crew – to share a Basra beyond the walls – a better Basra.

I have great memories of these calm evening walks. If we timed it well we would walk without body armour. Sometimes a colleague would jog past, red in the face and puffing out a highly disciplined routine of fitness – but my approach to health and welfare was gentler – Tai Chi, swimming and the occasional stroll. I painted pictures of the views in my pod and even wrote for a spiritual magazine when I returned to the UK about how I found peace and tranquillity in such unusual surroundings – you could never accuse me of not glossing over the terror.

Lock Down and the stolen sandwich

Another person not too bad at glossing over terror was Dr.
Kim Howells. I was researching and writing speeches for
him at the FCO a few months before I arrived in Iraq when
he spoke to the BBC Today programme: *"Iraq is a mess that
can't launch an attack now on Iran; a mess that won't be able
to march into Kuwait; it's a mess that can't develop nuclear
weapons. So yes it's a mess but it's starting to look like the
sort of mess that most of us live in"*. His words not mine, but
despite him being known as "Kim Howlers" at the FCO, I did
wonder in hope that Basra would indeed resemble a mess I
could live in.

Six months after Howell's bizarre assurance, I could feel
nothing but diminishment in the security situation. The
Foreign Office too, were soon to consider it a place that their
diplomats could no longer live in. My morale was being
chipped away at by both the regularity of attacks, and by the
confusion of responses by those at Basra Palace. Writing to
friends faded away and I had stopped telephoning home
every day. The gap between my reality in Basra and reality
elsewhere was growing.

During these difficult times, I did manage to hold a press
briefing. 15 Iraqi journalists risked their lives (some said) to
come to the Palace to meet our eloquent Ambassador,
Dominic Asquith as he visited Basra from Baghdad. Basra
often felt like the forgotten cousin, so any attention from a
Baghdad player was welcomed.

I had to grab hold of anything vaguely resembling success
with both hands. On the same day as the press conference
the media team suffered a blow as, despite our courting of
the military, I had word that our three high-level military
contacts had pulled out of a key meeting – with no
explanation or indication that they wished to continue the
conversation about strategy. It was not clear whether it was
a miscommunication or whether they had decided to opt out
of the whole coordinated-approach-to-communications thing.
Either way it was a setback. We still had the meeting, which
was reasonably fruitful: The Danish head of mission sat

next to me and picked holes in the language of the strategy document - he was right, actually – and we identified a need to quickly move on from writing this damn paper and begin actually doing something. I was ever impatient and was torn between cautious superiors insisting on word-perfect agreed strategy and different superiors who wanted action and quick wins. Often came the warning against weighing up whether one was "making a difference", but I couldn't help but consider if my efforts – all be it in dangerous circumstances – were actually worth it. The conclusion came in my diary (I was still writing, if not to friends back home): *"There are severe staff shortages - no one will volunteer to come out here and all local staff have left as one was shot and killed a few months ago. Due to this I fear that most of my time here will be spent fire-fighting'.*

The acknowledgement that strategy and progress would be difficult coincided with a decline in my health. Ghosts of a previous attack of shingles returned and seared pain into my back. Sleep deprivation was at last getting to me and my eyes were constantly bloodshot from air conditioning units and sand in the air - not too mention cigarette smoke, as I continued to up my nicotine intake.

On a particular low day I wrote about a mortar attack that *"thudded into the ground a few hundred metres away and sent me scurrying back to the cook-house"*. My main concern was not how close I was to losing my life, but the fact that the attack had meant another tedious lockdown. A day-time attack changed everything – and as Fridays were a nominal day off, it put a stop to any morale and health-boosting activity that might be planned. On that occasion we were stuck in lock down for over an hour. Swimming, walking, and being outdoors without body armour was immediately forbidden, so once the all clear sirens were heard, I scuttled back to my pod to try and catch up on lost sleep. I slept for about 10 minutes before I was called into the office.

There had been an incident involving some of our CRG security team. A convoy had been slugged with an IED. None were dead, but two were injured and one chap had to have his leg amputated a few hours later. When something like that happens, most people stop what they are doing and pause for reflection. My job was to prepare press lines with London and try and contact Baghdad, with whom, for some reason, we had lost all secure communications for 36 hours – I had to communicate with them using made up code over mobile phones. Having done all I could, finding myself at my desk (and giving up any notion of sleep) I decided to plough through the 300 emails that were sitting in my inbox. That evening, on my day off, I left my office at 8pm and headed straight for the bar, having missed supper and having only fire-fought my way through 200 of the emails.

Gloomily and hungrily, I shuffled across to the bar, feeling pleased still to have two legs, but nevertheless feeling pretty low. I ordered myself the last remaining sandwich in the place and popped to the toilet for a cigarette. When I returned to find that the grossly over-paid Justice Advisor had eaten half of my sandwich, it was the final straw. A trivial matter of course, but after a difficult day, tears began to sting my eyes as I mourned the loss of a sandwich (actually it was a Panini) and hated the Justice Advisor more than I had ever hated anyone before.

That night, breaking the no food in pods rule with a Pot Noodle, I wrote in my diary, *"I just wish they would stop bloody bombing us. The sooner they calm down, the sooner we will consider Basra "safe and ready for transition" and the sooner we can go.......can't they see that? Us civilians at the Palace are here to help this country back on its feet. I don't get why they want to bomb us every day. Frankly I am tired of it and want to go away. This time next week I should be in Kuwait.................boy I am ready for it"*.

One of the joys of being press officer was that whenever anything bad happened to a Brit, like the tragic attack on our convoy that lost one operative his leg, I would find myself immediately answering robust and aggressive questions about it – and sometimes the media would reach me with alarming speed. Following an attack, journalists' main concerns were a) had any Brits been killed? and b)

97

were any of those injured diplomats or high level officials? They almost seemed disappointed if a death were merely Iraqi or Sri Lankan or the lost leg belonged to a mere security guard and I think I actually swore down the line at one journalist who said "oh no-one important then". Bastards.

One occasion sticks in my mind, which I also believe proves Iran's involvement in the attacks against us. Late one morning I answered the phone to an AFP journalist based in Baghdad who said he had just heard that a diplomatic convoy in Basra City had been hit by an RPG and several British diplomats had been killed. I knew absolutely nothing about this, and made the usual promises to call back as soon as more was known. The BBC called, then CNN with the same query. I took my phone off the hook and immediately called our security team on the other phone - they knew nothing about the incident — but were understandably worried. We did have a team from the PRT visiting offices in the city, but last heard, they were quite well and safe. The security manager radioed to check.

The news was troubling, but I decided to wait a while before calling back the journalists to deny the story. Ten minutes later the security manager called me to say that the vehicle that our PRT colleagues were in had just come under an RPG attack. No-one had been killed, but one member of the close protection team had a face full of tiny pieces of shrapnel (nothing vision or life threatening). No-one else was close to being hurt, most of them were inside the building when it happened. The man who had fired the rocket had run off down an alleyway, and the security team had not felt it possible to pursue him. Their priority was the safe extraction of themselves and the PRT civilian staff from the situation. As he spoke, the whole group were safely on their way back to the Palace in a second vehicle — having abandoned the first. The big question that loomed for me was how *exactly* had journalists in Baghdad known about the event *before* it had happened? I picked up the phone.

It appeared that the inaccurate story was being spread about Baghdad news centres by the Basra based Iranian Al Alam stringer. It seemed fair to assume that if the stringer knew about the attack in advance — he was somehow complicit in the planning. Iranian and some Basra newspapers carried a photo-shopped picture of the attack on their front covers the following day. A grinning RPG-carrying "freedom fighter" standing next to a burning British wreck. It was complete fabrication. But carefully planned fabrication. And worse, a "strategic" fabrication.

Escape from Margaret Beckett on a Sea King

"I have never been afraid of the sky before – but I am here" – extract from my diary August 2006

In true Basra fashion, Britain's first female Foreign Secretary and her entourage were welcomed into town by a barrage of rockets. They all missed their target, but provided a backdrop of dramatic explosions - impressing our predicament upon the visitors. My task was to provide as much positive exposure to her visit in the Iraq media as possible.

Arranging for Ms Beckett to be interviewed on an Iraqi TV channel was more difficult than it sounds. On the day she was in town we also welcomed a sweaty, nervous Iraqi crew onto the compound and took them to the spot we had agonised over for the Foreign Secretary to be interviewed – a disused office on the ground floor of the PRT building.

Personally meeting journalists at the Saddam's Gate was important – I even went against rules and removed my body armour as we greeted. In my view wearing armour to welcome un-armoured guests gave a bad impression. These guests were already disgruntled, having waited in the sun, been questioned and searched and given up their mobile phones. They were always surprised and happy to see me there full of practiced *Salaams* and *Sabah Al-Chers* (thanks Jason) rather than the burly CRG security team who were their usual efficient but curt escort to the office. I even arranged for their equipment to be put into a truck and searched by the dogs separately, out of eyeshot. I loved the sniffer dogs (I think I mentioned my favourite, Debbie) who wore cute booties to stop their feet getting too hot. But they were less of a hit with some of the Iraqis.

This particular TV crew were jovial and excited at the prospect of meeting such a significant figure in the British Government. We scrabbled around at the last minute swapping the backdrop of real flowers for fake ones on the discovery of Ms. Beckett's allergy. We also miraculously found an eloquent English/Arabic speaker to act as interpreter – although Beckett didn't appear too accustomed to speaking through an interpreter and spoke too long in between pauses. We tried our best to operate with calm professionalism under the watchful eye of Beckett's Press Secretary.

Once done with the interview and egos nicely stroked, we had to escort the crew and all of their equipment off the base. But the crew seemed suddenly agitated at the thought of leaving; Ali, the young and funky TV presenter said he was worried that they had been followed to the Embassy Office that morning. It turned out that Ali spoke reasonable English (his colleagues not). He explained in stammers how his own interpreter had had his throat slit recently – he said he blamed Iranians. He said it was because they reported fairly, but were considered to be pro-British. I suddenly felt the almighty burden of having achieved what I thought was a media "success" for Ms Beckett and her UK government department – and realised that this was a life threatening assignment for Ali and his friends. I asked him if he intended to broadcast the interview. He reassured me he was – he wasn't wasting our time. I wasn't quite sure how reassured I felt by this.

A quick call to the security operations room revealed that the CCTV cameras had picked up a white Toyota that had appeared when the film crew arrived – and was still parked on the street outside our compound several hours later. I asked Ali. He didn't have a white Toyota – they had arrived by foot and walked a long way to avoid being followed. After a heated discussion with the crew Ali informed me that none of them wanted to leave the compound by the same gate they came in – they didn't trust the car. We then spent a significant amount of time weighing up which was the best possible way out. Our security staff were brilliant and thoroughly endorsed Ali's decision. They recommended that we use the American gate, which although exited into the city too, it was far enough away from the Toyota and close enough to access a taxi and make their escape.

Although right next to our camp, I hadn't spent much time on the US side. Their shop was disappointing and usually shut whenever I had the spare time to test it. It sold mostly brash Iraq *[eye-wrack]* branded T-shirts and baseball hats — the like of which had been useful only for costume parties. A couple of meals of French fries had been enjoyed in their cook-house, sitting uncomfortably beneath their "God Bless America" banner which swung overhead. I had a couple of friends on their base, but otherwise didn't know it well. We were soon to discover that the US compound perimeter was not guarded by smiling, efficient Nepalese.

The private security company employed by the Americans point blank refused to let the film crew onto the compound at first. We had a hard job persuading them that Ali and friends were merely trying to exit the compound. Trying to get them and their equipment out through the American gate was another matter — and it took tact, diplomacy, aggression, and finally bullying to allow them to be released into Basra City. Ali looked quite worried by my willingness to challenge the Americans — and I have to say looking into the steely eyes of a full blooded red-neck American complete with chewing gum and automatic weapon, to demand the free passage of a bunch of journalists was something I never thought I would have to do. They were trying to *leave* the compound for godsake (still makes me cross today).

The attitude of the Americans can be summed up by the warning sign printed on the back of their vehicles. It says "WARNING STAY BACK 100 METERS" in large red letters. The same is written in Arabic in white letters. The Arabic letters are smaller than the red letters and cannot be read from 100 metres. Nuff said. You have seen it on Youtube. Colleagues joked on our hostile territories training that our biggest threat to safety in Iraq came from Americans not Iraqis. It was rumoured that every private security detail knew that if you saw a US convoy, you stayed as far away from them as possible.

Thoughts of Ali's journey home via the American gate stayed with me throughout the day.

Back in Britain, Tony Blair was facing heavy criticism for not stating his date for leaving office and consequently his most loyal supporter, Ms Beckett had her mind on home politics. I hastily organised a down-the-line interview for her on BBC Radio Five Live in which she made only passing reference to being in Iraq. She filed her nails throughout the interview, and afterwards complained to me (randomly) about how "unsafe" using email was and moaned that she had nothing to wear when she had to make an unscheduled visit to a hospital in Jordan en route. Here is why she made the visit. Make your own mind up as to whether expressing her wardrobe quandary to staff in Basra was appropriate.

British tourist shot dead in Jordan

A British tourist died in a hail of bullets when a gunman chanting 'God is Greatest' opened fire at a group of horrified holidaymakers in Jordan on Monday.

Two British women were seriously injured when the lone killer pulled a pistol from his pocket and blasted off a dozen shots as they toured the popular Roman amphitheatre in the capital Amman.

Foreign Secretary Margaret Beckett said she was "extremely saddened" to learn of the shooting. "Acts of violence such as this are as senseless as they are callous," she said.

Source: Daily Mail – 4 September 2006

When she had finished with her string of complaints I took the opportunity to remind her of some of the difficulties we faced. I made sure she was aware that Ali and the TV crew had risked their lives to record her interview that day. I told her about his interpreter — about his slit throat. I told her about the way they had to leave the compound. Not that she asked, but I had a text from Ali later that night to say he had returned home safely. He thanked me. And sent me a short poem. It was the Iraqi way.

Exhausted and somewhat frustrated I left Basra city on the same evening as our esteemed Minister (but not on the same helicopter). The KBR manager, Chris, saw me off at the helipad and he joked, "don't go to the date palm farm" as we parted. He was referring to my very frequent requests to the security management team to go on visits out and about in Basra. The Security Manager *always* turned them down — having assessed the risks to my personal safety. My recent passion was to witness the replanting of the date palms — a PRT agricultural project that was an excellent reconstruction story I could share with visiting media, but I felt I needed to actually go there and see it, and photograph it, for myself. Many times I had my request to accompany various officials on a helicopter tour of the palms declined. It became a bit of a joke. One day I WILL get to the date palm farms for sure. One of the reasons for my date palm passion was a love of the fruit itself. I'd always seen dates as a dusty Christmas fruit with grotty stones and avoided them — but after a Basrawi journalist friend, Mahmood, brought me in a tray of delicious succulent dates and Philippa and I demolished the lot in a couple of hours - they are close to my heart and, where possible, my stomach.

My helicopter was not destined for the date palm farm that time, but instead I found myself once more at the Air Station. The next day, enjoying a transitory rest, I sat down to write the following diary entry, which still moves me today:

> *Supper at Basra Air Station was interrupted last night by a huge explosion as a mortar tore through a Land Rover parked about 100m away. The Justice Advisor (and bloody sandwich thief) sprinted with us at top speed into a small waist high bunker. Pouring in amongst the sandbags, we surprised ourselves by actually giggling, despite the danger. Can you imagine that? We were on an adventure - we even*

took photos of each other looking ridiculous. How the human brain copes with these things. I feel almost ashamed.

I have come to the end of my first six (seven?) weeks in Iraq and I am in transit – destination Kuwait – for my first R&R break. Most of my colleagues complain about the waiting around and needlessly complex route it takes to extract yourself from theatre (I am only travelling a few hours' drive down the road but it can take three days by air). However, as I sit on a very Foreign Office arm chair, caked in grime and sweat from passing travellers, I realise that this pause in my efforts to depart is a welcome one. I have a moment, a whole day if I am lucky, to gather my thoughts and reflect and anticipate before I am thrust into the bosom of my family, who eagerly await my arrival and will bowl me over with their concern for what type of person Iraq has made me.

As I sit amongst upholstered, faded FCO blue/green stripes (the type I have seen in Brussels, Bratislava and Bangkok) in an air-conditioned freight container, I see that this is the very first time I am really motivated to put pen to paper. Sure, I have sent a weekly message to my nearest and dearest, but my prose has been forced and I have relayed events very much with my audience in mind (as a true PR worker is wont). I have omitted my doubts and fears, the mortars and the morale-sapping security and management regimes at the Palace, to focus on surface stuff – the weather, the parties, the adventure of it all. I haven't bothered friends in my emails of any spiritual learning, revelations in self discovery or the now jaded mantra "am I making a difference"? – frankly, it would freak them out.

A huge white fridge full of blue plastic water bottles hums in the corner of this freight container, but not louder than the rattle of the air conditioning unit, which is clearly on its last legs, powered by the noisy generators outside. An urgent voice on BBC World (on top of the fridge) tells me of Blair's crisis back home. My eyelids droop and this filthy chair encourages sleep, but still I write. I'm hungry. It's 11am and I haven't eaten since a dry veggie burger I stuffed down as I stood next to Margaret Beckett last night, wondering whether she herself was "making a difference".

I have had a strange reaction this past week as colleagues have asked me questions like, "are you looking forward to seeing your family?" or "are you worried about the Foreign Secretary's visit tomorrow?" and "what are you doing with your R&R?" I realise that of all the places in the world, Iraq has taught me something I have been striving for all my life, and that is "to be here now". It sounds very John Lennon, I know, and even the new Consul General called me a "tree-hugger", but in this tough environment, where our colleagues get their legs blown off, soldiers get shot in the neck and Iraqi journalists get their throats slit, I have surprised myself by finding real spiritual clarity. I guess you call it "living for the moment", and I am not sure how sustainable this feeling would be in the real world, but right now I find this complete freedom from either nostalgia or anxiety of what's to come, the most liberating thing I have ever felt.

So in my comfy chair, in this freight container lidded with corrugated metal, situated in the dirty grounds of Britain's biggest military base in Iraq – Basra Air Station – I feel as free as a bird. The fact that this exhilaration moves me to tears is perhaps my only concern.

Later on the same day, driven by desire to express myself, I wrote again:

So I have filled my stomach with boiled dry rice and a husk of sweet bread in the cook-house. There is an obvious lack of vegetarians here, and as much as I find chickens loathsome and demonic, I can't bring myself to eat one. I'm back in my chair. It's bloody hot out there, at least 45 degrees (here I go with the weather again, I need to dig deeper). Being a female out here is odd, but does have its advantages. If I was a male civilian ambling my way to the cook-house in the midday sun, I doubt I would be so quickly befriended. I always have entertaining dining company as the men folk use the opportunity of a female ear to display their wit and relate amusing tales of bravado. They are also intrigued by the WFAIDI factor (What the Fuck Am I Doing in Iraq). I was joined at lunch today by a familiar face, Graham from CRG (whose name has been changed to protect his identity), who rather uncomfortably refers to us Foreign Office staff as "clients". He will be travelling with me this evening as we wind our way across the oil fields of the south in a Sea King Helicopter – me into the arms of my family and him on a welfare break after helping to save the life of his colleague who lost his leg when the convoy he was travelling in was hit by a road side bomb. A brave man indeed.

I have at least six hours before that flight and I am considering a post lunch snooze. Being in Iraq is very much like having a new born baby – undisturbed sleep becomes the most precious commodity. I have Mark Etherington's book "Revolt on the Tigris" by my side and I promised myself to make a start on this written tale of Etherington life "back in the CPA days", having heard snippets from him in the bar. Etherington (or "Bemused of Hastings" as he calls himself in emails) is an eloquent and charming man (Google him – quite a guy), together with his beautiful partner, Emma, (beautiful in body and spirit I hasten to add) they make the most attractive and envied pair in town. The only pair, actually. If Hello magazine did Basra, I am sure they would feature pictures of the two of them reclining on their Foreign Office sofas in their pod.

I could stroll across to the Naafi for chocolate or some cheap pirate DVDs, but I don't fancy donning body armour, and as comfortable as I now feel in the 98% male dominated environment at the Palace, I feel strangely unnerved surrounded by heat stressed soldiers here at the airport.

I spoke to Foreign Secretary Beckett about the male dominated environment thing yesterday. She gave me the "get on with it girl" line and compared it to working in Parliament where there are loads of blokes apparently. I wanted to say "yeah, but they don't carry automatic weapons around Westminster and they go home at night and shag their wives (or whatever)". But instead we spoke about the trials of putting on make up, doing your hair (a-hem Margaret) and finding the right outfit to wear when visiting gunned down tourists in hospital in Amman. Bless her, her mind is back in the UK...........who gives a shit about Basra when the PM's leadership is under threat?

When Sir John and the Iraq Inquiry team asked about the value of Ministerial visits four years later, you can imagine my response. Beckett was more than an irritation in Basra – but then again, maybe I wasn't in the best place to receive her. I was an efficient but not graceful host. Remarkably I unearthed my weekly email from the time, in which I complained about being fed up with my clothes as "most of them seemed to be perpetually lost in the laundry" and moaned that my Marks & Spencer's order hadn't arrived. No mention at all of exploding Land Rovers or limbless security guards. There's a Beckett in me yet – maybe she was doing a fair amount of gloss herself during her visit. For all I knew she was terrified.

One thing I find astounding when I look back is that during the ten day break ahead of me in Kuwait – I actually reasonably considered that I could learn Arabic in this time. Perhaps I was banking on sticking to the four hours sleep a night regime – but even then it was a slightly unrealistic ambition! On safer ground I wrote once more to my friends from Kuwait:

11 September 2006

(five years on and the world is a safer place....a-hem)

Dearest friends of Bourn,

I did say I wouldn't write for a few weeks, but I thought I would drop you a quick line, on this very special anniversary, to say that I am just fine and dandy and enjoying myself in sunny Kuwait.

I left Basra Palace a few hours later than Margaret Beckett after she and I had shared a glass or two of Jacobs Creek. She was anxious about Tony back home and I was getting my usual helicopter jitters. As it was, I left Iraq on an exhilarating ride across a darkened desert on a Sea King along with some military top brass. I must say, I prefer the Merlin, but the view out of the cockpit (do heli's have cockpits?), of the front chopper in our convoy silhouetted against the full moon was rather special. I rocked up at our Kuwait City apartment nastily sweaty, but happy to be alive.

The kids are amazingly settled into school here. Daisy has impressed me with her Arabic homework (better than my own) and Vin and Billy think that school is "wicked" and seem to have a nice routine of an early start, a lunch time finish, followed by a swim in our pool and the usual relaxing techniques (Playstation, movies, fighting with each other). Peter facilitates all

110

of this with ease and knows his way around Kuwait like a Palestinian taxi-driver.

It's quite unbelievable to think that just a few hours away from this decadent multi-cultural life in Kuwait awash with enough Lamborghinis, Ferraris and private yachts to make you weep, Basrawis are verging on civil war (there, I said it) and scrap around in violent poverty. Not so long ago Kuwaitis would escape this place and holiday in Basra – the Venice of the Middle East. One can only hope we can give them the capacity to reassemble that dream. (Bloody hell – hark at me? Enough already.)

So. Kuwait. It is so civilized it is revolting.

Perhaps a little too much analysing the situation........need to get my Bourn Girls head back on and get down the salon again for a wax, massage and a haircut. Plenty of wine flowing from the Embassy bar into my apartment and Belgian chocolates, so I have no excuse to be anything but shallow.

More rantings next week, when I get back behind the Iraqi curtain........

xxxxxxxxxxx

PS - Janet – The Pod is firmly above ground, sorry to disappoint. Crete sounds wonderful and a million miles away from anywhere near here, although the Bo Dereks put me off. If you want to raise your self-esteem come live in a camp that is 98% male – after a few weeks, you too will look like Bo Derek.

But despite seeing my wonderful, resilient, clever, loving children – and having some degree of pampering (very odd seeing Burkha clad women arrive at the beautician's and strip off to reveal jeans, full face make-up and general groovy funkiness) the rest and recuperation break wasn't exactly that.

An old American friend who also lived in Kuwait gave me the nod that all was not well with Peter and it was clear that he was not coping with me being away. Peter and I argued. He decided to start smoking (as I had) and was drinking more than two cans a day I fear. He felt abandoned and not needed. Yet in reality I needed him more than ever before – just not in the way he was used to – I needed him to be rock strong for me. We felt like strangers to one another. He felt very sorry for himself and thought me selfish (a fair accusation maybe) and I felt very, very angry at the lack of support (and thought him selfish). We were at odds.

Our marriage did not survive the posting to Iraq, and although me going there was clearly not the entire cause of our split (which, looking back, had seen cracks appear for years before) it certainly put the pressure on and speeded up the process. I instigated our parting not long after our final return to Britain and because of this (and because of the extraordinary adventure I was on) I felt the guilt of this as a heavy burden for some time to come.

It was under this cloud that I sat on the balcony of our Kuwait apartment waiting for the Embassy vehicle to collect me to take me back into theatre. Both Peter and I were chain smoking and unsure how to part. All sorts of demons were emerging for him, and I attempted some inadequate reassurances – but my mind was on that word "try" I had heard once more down the phone moments earlier. The Embassy were going to "try" to get me back to Basra by road again. Closed for weeks before, they thought the road route might be safe again. I felt like a perpetual guinea-pig for the IED ridden Tampa Route. And this time I had a far more acute sense of the dangers I faced. Frankly, I didn't really want to go.

The Tampa Route

A few days after my son's 8th birthday in September 2006 I was taken by road from the Kuwait border up the Tampa route towards the Air Station in Basra. As before, an eight person Close Protection and Counter-attack Team accompanied me back to Basra. It was a real contrast to my first arrival in Iraq a couple of months prior, where I gazed in wonder at the bizarre remains of concrete picnic tables that lined the main supply route north through the flat desert and oil fields. This time many of the security team were known to me by face if not by name. Graham, the guy I had travelled out of Iraq with on the General's Sea King helicopter was amongst them. He was the one who administered first aid to our man who had lost his leg in an IED attack a few weeks earlier. We exchanged pleasantries at the arid border post and stamped out our cigarettes before crossing into Iraq. I was definitely back to being a "client" and quickly realised that some of the thoughts he had shared about his experience were now out of bounds - Graham was at work. He did mention that on his R&R he had been to visit his amputee friend in hospital in Birmingham and that he was recovering well. This was Graham's first tasking since he'd returned. One had to admire the resilience of this group of men.

As we trekked up the Tampa route in our armoured jeep the driver suddenly became agitated and although I didn't even notice, it appeared a tyre had blown out on our vehicle. Our four-vehicle convoy screeched to a tactical stop. I glanced over to Graham – very aware that in the moments before the roadside bomb tore his friend's leg off, they too had stopped to change a tyre. He must have been reliving some horrors, but didn't show it.

Myself and the police trainer travelling with me, were expertly "cross-decked" into another vehicle, and amazingly, tyre changing on a jeep weighing a few tons was done with Formula 1 precision and within less than four minutes we were back moving on the road. I had felt very vulnerable whilst we were waiting on the quiet desert road. The term

113

"sitting ducks" springs to mind. The radio crackled the moment we stopped, "Kilo, you are static, is everything ok?" Nice to know that somewhere in Iraq we were being tracked. Graham and his team patrolled on the road outside with automatic weapons and I was struck by how many of them had shaved their heads. Baldies shining in the blistering midday Iraq heat - despite their bullet proof coats, weaponry and body-builder physiques the lack of hair struck me as a peculiar vulnerability. Wittering small-talk to the police trainer in the back of the vehicle, I managed to keep myself relatively stress free and calm.

The rest of the journey went without incident and I was thrilled (ecstatic is fair) to find Etherington's lovely Emma and the gorgeous Tash huddled in a Red Sea freight container at the Air Station. It was great to see them; we chatted and caught up on some camp gossip and more on political developments of the past fortnight. They confirmed what I had been hearing from the Embassy in Kuwait – that IDF attacks on the Palace had increased. We had supper in the make-shift cook-house and sat around in white plastic chairs as we drank a tentative pre helicopter-ride beer. We got the lads to take pictures of us all together draped over a CRG jeep - the girls back home would have been proud.

Despite my tortured departure from Kuwait, my mojo had returned and I was feeling special, smart, daring and on a worthwhile mission once more. Perhaps the R&R really had done what it said on the tin.

Baha, Julio and Saman

"We have done exactly what it said on the tin" - Tony Blair on allegations that he has betrayed Labour's traditional values, August 2006.

I flew back into the Palace with the lovely Emma and although I didn't see much of her after my return, we occasionally caught each other's eye in the cook-house and knew we were allies. As we landed that night we saw tracer rise into the sky and had barely set foot in the Palace compound before a mortar explosion shook the ground around us – it was not a good start back! The CRG security chap who collected us in the "happy bus" from the helipad was wearing a helmet and body armour himself – the first time I had seen that, so I knew the reports of increased "activity" were true.

Apparently British Troops had (accidentally) killed a terrorist who had tried to defend himself as they arrested him (don't read sarcasm into the "accidentally" bit - I am convinced it was). But rumours about town were that we had executed him at the Palace – hence his men were retaliating with an increase in attacks. Something else that didn't help was the court martial of British soldiers back in the UK. At least one had pleaded guilty to treating Iraqi prisoners inhumanely, the justification appeared to be that life was tough in Basra:

Bleak in Basra, court martial told

The commanding officer of British soldiers accused of war crimes in Iraq admitted there were bound to be times when the harsh conditions his men worked in got the better of them, a court martial heard yesterday.

Colonel Jorge Mendonca said the troops faced a constant threat of attack, worked as many as 20 hours a day and could not sleep in the sweltering heat during their brief breaks. Four of Col Mendonca's soldiers are accused of abusing Iraqi prisoners, while he and two other officers face charges of failing to make sure the detainees were treated properly... The court martial has heard that the soldiers in charge of the Iraqis may have treated them badly partly because they were suspected of involvement in the killing of six members of the Royal Military Police and were upset at the death of one of their colleagues, Captain Dai Jones.

It has been alleged that the civilians were hooded, deprived of sleep and forced to maintain illegal "stress positions" - all banned interrogation techniques. The ill-treatment culminated in the death of one of the Iraqis, hotel worker Baha Mousa.

Source: Steven Morris, Guardian, Saturday September 23, 2006

Not surprisingly the Iraqi media hadn't been covering the long hours, soaring temperatures, and danger that British soldiers faced so much and focused mostly on human rights abuses. Interesting to see the use of sleep deprivation as torture. I can tell you it's VERY effective.

So as a result of all this we were put on Alert State 3 — the highest level — from the moment I returned from R&R. It was more the alert state and not the actual attacks which caused most damage to morale. I complained in an email to friends — not of the threat to my life caused by mortar showers but that I had bought a new swimming costume whilst I was in Kuwait and hadn't had the chance to wear it: *"the pool stays closed and any movement out of doors is in full body armour, helmet and quickly. Lack of sunshine on the skin in a sunny country is draining"*. With the majority of attacks taking place at night, we had all begun to question the necessity of the level 3 Alert Status. And then we suffered our first civilian fatality.

One Friday afternoon, on our nominated day of rest, a rocket scored a direct hit into the flimsy living accommodation on the US side - just a few hundred yards down the track. It killed one American civilian, Julio Garcia, immediately. No one else was injured. We were stunned. Our American colleagues were mortified.

It dominated my work for the next 24 hours and although I had only just arrived back, morale sank to below previous levels, and I wrote in my diary, *"I finally admit that I am thoroughly pissed off living in this place, trying to do a job whilst others try to murder me"*.

The US State Department issued a statement, which I spun out to the British media with a lump in my throat:

> *It is with a profound sense of sadness and regret that we announce the loss of a State Department contractor as the result of a rocket attack in Basra, Iraq on September 22, 2006.*
>
> *As a member of our Embassy community, this American citizen worked toward assisting the people of Iraq build a stable, democratic, and prosperous country.*
>
> *On behalf of the U.S. Embassy and the entire American community in Iraq, I would like to extend our deepest sympathy to the family and friends of our colleague.*

Later the same day, the US side was hit by a further two rockets – there were no casualties this time, although their bar was hit. Cynically and curiously as I read the US Press Statement I found myself questioning the reference to "democracy" and wondered whether this word had been overused and was therefore meaningless in today's world. There was a realisation that perhaps I was doing a job here that was made for me – and no matter what crisis and sadness was at hand, I could manage to see through it and do my work.

Still in a state of shock I tried to write to the girls back in the quiet sleepy village, if only to let them know that I was safe and not to scare them too much.

My dear, dear friends of Bourn in England,

Today's report from the Basra Big Brother house comes to you with a sense of sadness, but you should know I am perfectly safe. See below:

A U.S. contractor working for the American consulate in Iraq's second biggest city, Basra, was killed by a rocket that struck the main British compound in the city overnight, U.S. and British officials said on Saturday.

The missile struck the Basra Palace compound, a riverside marble Palace of former ruler Saddam Hussein, which is guarded by Britain and houses some of its troops as well as diplomatic missions for Britain, the United States and their allies.

The Palace is regularly targeted with rockets and mortars, but this was the first fatality reported inside the heavily fortified compound. The U.S. State Department confirmed the death but did not say what the contractor's job was.

British forces are responsible for the mainly-Shi'ite southern sector of Iraq and are concentrated mainly around Basra, with three small bases inside the city and one at an airport outside it.

Major Charlie Burbridge, a British military spokesman, said the three bases in the city were usually struck "two nights in three" by volleys of rockets or mortars, but the strikes rarely cause damage.

"It's not overwhelming, but it is something we've been putting measures in place to deal with," he said.

Source: Reuters, 23rd September 2006

After opening my message with this cheerful news report, I continued, astonishingly, without further reference to Julio. Instead, I told them that Charlie Burbridge was an arse, complained again about the lack of new swimming costume opportunity and responded to my friends in what I thought was a witty and individual way.

Alison - My God! Your house caught fire! Do be careful with your lava lamps darling. I am still waiting for the photos of you all with the Gamlingay Fire Crew to adorn my pod. Perhaps we should set up a twinning programme Bourn and Basra – with fires and electricity black outs there is a lot in common. In fact, I have been asked to look into Iraqi Women's Groups at work, so there could be a sister group to ours in the making.

Rob – No, I am not going to film me puking on a helicopter. Honestly

Lorna – I really think you should consider selling your body if those green suede cowboy boots from Jigsaw are what you really want. Your mention of back, sack & crack waxing reminds me to let you know how staggered I am at the many, many blokes here who don't just shave their heads, but their chests too....I mean.....is that right?

Julia – Another new au pair? Always best to get one that knows the right way around round-abouts. I was confused about the new cost saving idea at your work – you could always try threatening to shoot a member of staff – it's seems to free up desks in no time here.

119

My message ends with bizarre reassurance that I would be back in Bourn at the beginning of November for R&R. And I promised that I would write a wonderfully upbeat message the following week: *"who knows, peace may have broken out in the Middle East by then and I may be able to go shopping in down town Basra and take a booze cruise up the Shatt Al-Arab"*.

This message above all others demonstrates a need to reassure friends back home, however, I'm not convinced that my chirpy quips on a day when we had our first fatality did the trick. I'm still not sure how this was received back home; it feels woefully inappropriate. I'd like to note here that the "Charlie is an arse" comment was aimed at undermining Charlie's less than encouraging and inadequate assessment of attacks on the Palace in his statement. If my words were inappropriate, then his "it's not overwhelming" on the day Julio died, were woefully misplaced. Perhaps I was just irked by Charlie's lack of enthusiasm for my silly civvy communications strategy and his boasts at being the 5th most quoted man in the world.

About a week later the US Embassy Office held a memorial service for Julio. It was a very strange affair. Philippa and I went along. I had uncannily remembered to bring something black back from Kuwait with me – I didn't realise I'd be needing it in a matter of days. We were in fact the only ones wearing black, and stood uncomfortably sombre amongst our gum-chewing colleagues, who were dressed in primary coloured T-shirts. Our presence at the ceremony was much welcomed and we suddenly felt a closeness to our American colleagues like never before. Bizarrely every one of the attendees (about 100 of us), including the minister carrying out the service, was wearing body armour – many with helmets too. The service was inside, but the cover was "soft" and not "hard" and we were still at level 3 alert.

Julio's death made everything suddenly personal. A young man relaxing on his bed, perhaps reading a magazine or watching a DVD, when a rocket tore through him. He wasn't a soldier. He wasn't there to fight – but to support. And I know you could argue that soldiers were there to reconstruct too – but the fact is they were trained killers and joined the military fully expecting combat. I know that my military colleagues were bitter about a civilian's life appearing to mean more than their own in the eyes of the media – though I have never once felt any difference in the level of loss, whoever was killed; but Julio's death brought the danger closer to *me*. Up until then I had felt invincible. Let's face it; we were entirely vulnerable, unarmed, untrained, civil servants – quite unused to such an environment. I was also well aware that the loss of a diplomat could well spell the end of civilian involvement in southern Iraq – something the military were keen to impress as crucial to reconstruction.

On the same day as Julio died a Danish security officer named Kim working out of the tiny Danish Office was also killed. And a few days later a British private security officer shot himself somewhere outside of Basra. Having lost my first husband through suicide, this was a tough one to handle – and as my telephone began to ring once more with journalists eager for inside news on all three deaths, the pressure increased again.

At around about the same time, the Iraqi and British military launched a big operation in Basra, with the hope of "clearing the streets" (I was still thinking marigold gloves and bin liners). Actually "clearing the streets" is probably a bit basic – it actually involved crashing into areas, clearing rubbish, painting and repairing schools and hospitals. Oh... and getting rid of the death squads within the Iraqi police force. It was all good morale boosting stuff, but not without its problems. The push (under the *Better Basra* plan) also involved a huge amount of media work and promotion of reconstruction.

3,000 British troops try to tame Basra

The British Army deployed thousands of troops on to Basra streets yesterday in an operation to re-establish

121

*control over a city that has been swept by a wave of
lawlessness and militia infiltration.*

*Ministry of Defence officials said 3,000 British
soldiers, a third of whom were dispatched into the city
with 2,000 Iraqi troops, were engaged in Operation
Sinbad, an ambitious campaign to rid the city of its
thieves and rogue officials.*

*They will also work with local officials and
communities to tackle problems ranging from
organised crime to poor infrastructure.*

Source: Telegraph, 28 September 2006

I wrote in my diary: *"I am strangely comforted by the sounds
of ambulance and police sirens outside the compound walls –
I think it means that the emergency services in Basra are
beginning to work. Less comforting is the daily dull
slamming of mortars which continue to plague us".*

And there was no let up. Charlie's assessment of two attacks
in every three days was soon laughable. We received
incoming IDF (either a barrage of rockets or two or three
mortars) every day and every night – often many times
within 24 hours. Everyone felt that it was just a matter of
time before someone on the Foreign Office compound was
killed or injured. The military camp (next door) was struck –
soldiers were injured as we heard the doors being blown off
their main building.

Late one evening, several close explosions rocked my pod. I
thought the windows would crack and could only wait for the
continuing barrage to hit my temporary home head on. But
it didn't come. Instead amongst the deafening sirens and
Tannoy instructions, my phone rang and it was Saman, my
Sri Lankan friend from the kitchens. Miraculously a rocket
had hit his Red Sea container home he shared with another
Sri Lankan cook. It was a "blind" rocket (it failed to explode)
and had continued on through his small room and exited on
the opposite wall (and ended up buried deep in the supply

stores). Their eardrums were blown out and they had minor cuts and bruises but they survived this attack. I knew in Sri Lanka Saman would be considered very lucky and auspicious, people would want his blessing as a miraculous survivor and I told him so. But he was very scared.

When I visited them in the clinic the next day Saman and his friend were in sheepishly good spirits. They wanted to stay at the Palace, but were being sent to Shaiba hospital for a check up. Unlike my pathetic swimming pool bump, their blood caked ears betrayed some real war injuries – yet they still felt like frauds alongside soldiers.

Saman's gentle spirit, his bravery, and laid back humour in the face of adversity moved me then, as does the memory of him today.

Sadly, Saman's luck did not last and he was killed by a mortar at the Air Station some time later. Despite his culinary skills, he had taken a job as a security guard whilst the new FCO kitchens were being built at the air base. A mortar hit the guard hut he sat in and killed him outright. My friend Chris, the KBR manager is troubled deeply by Saman's death to this day. It was he that arranged his temporary security assignment, away from the kitchens. Chris is still working in Iraq at the time of writing this and has visited my beloved Sri Lanka to meet Saman's family. The ripples of hurt that are caused by a single death travel far and wide. In places like Iraq, when so many people are killed, the ripples must become waves.

Zen and the art of rockets and mortars

The two-can rule continued to be abused and avoided - much to the annoyance of the management and security teams. The problem was that whilst threats to have you thrown off camp could control the FCO staff (of which there were only nine!), the rest of the compound were from a range of different countries and governments and plenty of them were contractors who knew their worth (the sandwich thief, it was rumoured, was on a thousand pounds a day!) The Danes, as mentioned, flouted the rule by holding drinks at dusk parties, but they felt they had good reason — they had a small community and one of them, Kim had been killed. I was always impressed however, at their fair mindedness and general resilience to alcohol — but I do remember one Danish friend, a blond policeman (who remains nameless) commiserating the loss of Kim in the bar and expressing his often mooted desire to invade Kuwait with "a mere handful of Danish special forces". We had heard that rant in the smoking room many times before but never so passionately. A glimpse of a man so angry with the world and uncharacteristically emphatic for a Scandinavian. He seemed to have stopped calling everyone stupid by the next morning over a black coffee at breakfast, but despite his claims to be un-emotional, his hurt at the loss of his friend was plain to see.

Eventually, having been given the go-ahead by the security team to rid ourselves of body armour and helmets for the first time in ten days and desperate for some exercise there was a race on for the cool relief of the pool. I for one was thrilled at the chance to be outside and active. I missed swimming, and I had previously been doing 30 lengths a day. The beautiful, tranquil, turquoise waters were only to be avoided during squaddie hours, when bombing of a different kind was common. My only exercise of late had been the frequent lifting of a cigarette to my mouth and the tapping of fingers across my computer keyboard. There was a gym on camp — but the very idea that I might exert myself alongside a group of shaved body-obsessed security/police/prisons staff was laughable.

I'm still not sure why we all considered the drop of alert status as proof that we would be safe – but I think the security team were well aware of the effect on morale that the level 3 status was having. Plus they had nowhere to escalate to if things got even worse – level 3 was the top. Some people mooted that the level 3 was temporarily dropped because the security manager wanted to go for a jog. Who cared? I was going swimming and I made every effort to be the first in the water!

Wearing nothing more than my carefully-selected, dowdy, black swimming costume from Kuwait (at last!) I found myself completely alone at the swimming pool. I had got there first as planned, but as I dipped my big toe into the water, disturbing the surface for the first time in over a week, a Katyusha rocket came urgently rushing overhead. Looking up to see the missile, it seemed unreal - almost like a cartoon - and felt close enough to reach out and touch. I froze and with only my eyes moving in my head I followed its trajectory and heard (and felt) it explode a short distance away, sending up a puff of smoke (and injuring several soldiers and taking out a vehicle, I was later to discover). The water in the pool rippled in response. My reaction was bizarre and still makes me smile as I write this. I gasped like a child and might have uttered "oooops", then covered my breasts with my hands (despite having a costume on) in a very Barbara Windsor *Carry-On* moment and then scuttled to the only reinforced space nearby – a very small room which housed a fridge filled with water bottles. As I waited for the next rocket to appear (as they usually came in batches of at least three) I peered from my place of cover out at the sky. But no more came and the sirens reminded me that I needed to let security know I was unharmed. So, against the rules, I scrambled to my radio and cell phone which lay next to a sun lounger and scampered back into the tiny pool room. After ten minutes of waiting in the small space in soaring temperatures with only the sound of my beating heart and the gentle lapping of the enticing waters to keep me company I decided to go back to my room. So, laden with my body armour (which I carried rather than putting on for no real reason I can think of), towels, my book, bag, and communications equipment I shuffled home in a rather comic way, walking just with the lower half of my legs as my sarong was slipping into the dust.

Letting out a big sigh, I clunked the heavy metal door of my pod closed behind me. As the air conditioning had been off, my room was a hot house. So much for the refreshing dip. I hoped the security manager had managed to jog for a minute, at least.

I think it was from that moment on that I learnt to be afraid of the sky. I'm not sure why it was on this particular occasion — experts would say my "bravery bank" had been used up. But once you actually see a loaded bomb flying through the air, hear its impact and the shudder of the ground, then even a swooping sparrow caught in peripheral vision can make you flinch. It also took several months back home before I ceased to start at a slamming door and a back-firing car saw me on the floor.

During that same week I was caught outside again during an attack. It's so much worse outside — the dull thuds become deafening smacks, accompanied by the pattering of sand and shrapnel for minutes after. We were obviously back on high alert and outside activity was once again forbidden. We did however sometimes *have to* move around from place to place — from office to pod, from pod to cook-house, etc. This was done quickly and with body armour and helmet. I was walking from my office with Jawwad — a wonderful colleague with whom Jason and I shared an office. Jawwad was calm, cool and collected in a very measured way (unlike young Chris who had been just pure dude with his coolness). Again, I am sure Jawwad was my junior in terms of years, but he seemed to be spiritually mature beyond his years. If anyone could have persuaded me to convert to Islam it was he — he set such a fine example. I also enjoyed his sense of humour and many a laugh was shared. Jawwad was a big fan of my silly cartoon drawing and contributed many of the ideas. His pod backed onto mine and we would bang coded messages through the wall to each other at night during attacks, each giggling to ourselves at the ridiculousness of our predicament.

Jawwad and I were ambling along to the cook-house for lunch when we were caught in a mortar attack. Mortars made a different sound to rockets and three impacted loudly around us. Rather than throw ourselves to the ground, the pair of us ran the last few metres at top speed and burst in on the crowded diners, panting back our breath and pale with fright. That was when I realised quite how well soundproofed our hard cover buildings were; a few of our colleagues looked up from their plates with mild concern at our expressions, but amazingly no one had even heard the crashing explosions outside. Only when the sirens started up did they groan at the thought that they would be stuck for what turned out to be an hour, until the all clear was given. Jawwad of course – shaken but not stirred, ran his hands over his bald head and grinned – at least we could have a decent lunch break.

With an increase in attacks, sleep deprivation was becoming a problem for many. I prided myself in the training that having three children had provided. I could wake, feed, and change a baby and quickly slip back into a deep sleep. It is perhaps the ultimate test – to be woken every few hours, reduced to a zombie-like state and yet be solely responsible for the fragile well-being of a tiny infant. I was interested to read some research, which revealed that although pregnant women undergo a phase of so-called "baby brain", when they experience an apparent loss of function, this is because their brains are being remodelled and prepped for motherhood so that they are able to cope with the many new demands they will experience - changes that include improved cognitive abilities. So there is even scientific evidence that mothers have enhanced capacity to deal with challenging environments.

Despite acknowledging the strengths that being a mother brought, I tried my very best not to think about my children during those days in Iraq. This was part of a very conscious toughening up exercise I was putting myself through. The pictures they had drawn for me and photographs of them lay face down in my drawer – I tried having them on the walls for a while, but their lovely faces disturbed me. Talking to them on the phone was difficult and despite trying to speak to them each day, it was avoided towards the end, because keeping upbeat was near impossible. My biggest fear, as I lay alone at night, was that I would be killed, leaving my children motherless. However, my feelings were that if I were to survive this, a remarkable example would be set for all my children, but for my daughter most. As danger increased, however, my mission felt less noble and it dawned on me that it was no coincidence that I was the only mother there – other mothers were quite responsibly out of harm's way.

The increased accuracy of attacks meant that we did more than answer the role call on the radios when an explosion was heard – we often donned our helmets and stayed nervously awake wondering whether the next impact point would spell the end. Many of us took to the safety of our small bathrooms at night. Half asleep, I would sit slumped in my body armour on my bathroom floor with my mobile and radio in my hand. Other times it was about finding things to occupy and distract myself - eating a Pot Noodle at about three in the morning and quite often painting my toe nails (note: I had a helmet on but bare feet; that seems wrong, looking back). Usually I switched off the radio, so as to avoid hearing the crackle of our attackers, who sometimes broadcast shouts of *"allahu akbar"* to accompany the incoming ordnance. I felt like Margaret Thatcher – often getting by with four hours sleep a night (similarity ends there I hope).

Tempers were getting frayed by the sleep problems. On one occasion I visited the "Basra Hilton" - a band of four inmates had given their grouped pods hotel status and even had a guest book to sign. They had set up a golf driving range (if memory serves me right) – but with no outside activity allowed, the plastic grass sat dormant and dusty. As I walked into one of the crowded pods the atmosphere was charged – people were drinking (naughty, naughty) and the voices of Australian and Danish contractors could be heard above the crowd. It appeared that the poor, knackered, security manager had implid in a joke over the Tannoy that the Danes were perhaps not obeying the two-can rule. Imagine. I thought it was quite funny – but a combination of tiredness and danger blew throw-away comments way out of proportion. I felt like a school mistress walking into a classroom of excitable children egging on an angry kid. They might as well have been saying "Fight! Fight! Fight!". With a natural aversion to such confrontations, my instinct was to try and smooth things over between the warring parties. Eventually the situation was resolved without major diplomatic incident – but it demonstrated how petty things were getting and perhaps how the role of a mother-figure was never more relevant.

Despite the sleepless nights and the hugely frustratingly unsatisfying workload, there was a sense of becoming somehow stronger. Much of this was thanks to Tai Chi. After a year of classes back home, finally I had been able to perfect my ten minute form whilst in Basra. When I first arrived I scoured the camp looking for suitable places to practice. Sometimes I would visit an empty room in the block that housed the gym. I'd sneak in with a bottle of water and shut the door behind me – but it felt a bit prison-like and I always had half an eye on the door for fear that some burly security man would burst in and "find" me. In the end my form was practiced in my room with the help of Mike Tabbrett's manual (albeit a bit crumpled) and my new skills were unveiled every morning at 6am on a perfect sandy spot next to the lake.

The view from there was beautiful and sometimes a sunrise was witnessed, which turned the sandy buildings and muted palms into silhouettes against the Basra sky. Bee-eater birds would swoop around the man-made lake and often one of the stray cats would rub around my legs as I warmed up for my form with some quiet Chi Qong exercises. It was by far the best start to the day and I honestly don't think I could have got through living in Basra without it. Although we were sometimes confined to rooms before 6.30 so routes could be cleared by Debbie and her doggie friends, I would sneak out, walking barefoot through the quiet camp to ensure I began the day spiritually at peace. I was never once disturbed by IDF on these pilgrimages and only the odd passing early morning lake jogger even noticed I was there.

The golf cart/Warrior ratio

It wasn't all Zen and mortars – life in Basra was frequently filled with uncontrollable laughter. I drew cartoons mocking the rules, we wrote pub quizzes that were specifically aimed at challenging the military by quizzing them on their own stuff, and I even found myself in one humorous moment as the highest-ranking diplomat there, which technically meant I was in charge. My feet up on the Consul-General's desk, I gave everyone the day off at the morning meeting – which made everyone laugh, as we all knew there was in practice no such thing.

In amongst this danger and angst, media visitors were still arriving (and I was still developing the bloody strategy). It felt as if BBC correspondent Paul Wood practically lived at the Palace (and avoided being escorted at every opportunity). Paul often stayed in my room – which was by far the most pleasant, as I had pictures Blu-tacked to the walls and candles and scarves littered about the place. I hasten to add that I didn't *share* with Paul - I was able to use Jason's pod or another pod vacated during R&R breaks. It was probably not Paul's ideal gritty war-time experience, but at least I knew he was comfortable – and I knew where he was (most of the time).

As if to evidence my connection with the news they were reading back home, I wrote to my Bourn friends: *"My friend Paul Wood filed a report about trouble in Amara whilst sitting on the wall outside our cook-house this evening...here is the breaking news on the BBC as I write this:"*

> ### UK may return to Iraq crisis city
> *British troops remain on standby to help out Iraqi forces in Amara after an outbreak of serious violence. The Army said the southern city was "calm but tense" after hundreds of extra Iraqi troops were sent there. Clashes between police and up to 300 gunmen on Thursday and Friday left at least 30 people dead and 100 injured. The UK handed power to Iraqi forces in Amara in August. The country's foreign ministry is*

now calling for a rethink of the police of transferring power.

I'd lost my media massive – Dieter was safely back in Plymouth, Jason on R&R and David...well he slipped in and out of theatre like the enigmatic Aussie he was. I was on my own mainly, but I drew both the lovely Jawwad and young enthusiastic Chris in to help where possible. My friendship with Olivia, who was press liaison on the military side paid off and we worked far better together at coordinating visits. But despite improved coordination, I was becoming ever cynical about my mission. I wrote flatly in my diary: *"This week I held a press conference with my Iraqi journalist friends and was pleased to make it at least to the front pages of a few Iraqi Newspapers and the local TV station lead their news item with their interview with the Consul General. Despite these relative successes I still feel like I am treading water in a very deep ocean as far as real engagement with the locals goes".*

The press conference was no mean feat – so it is very sad that I felt I was merely treading water. Getting any amount of Iraqis onto the compound required hours of work – form filling, security checks, lists of names, quibbles over cameras and equipment. But it was fun in a way, and I was getting to know the journalists better and better despite the language barriers, which were worse when Jason was away of course. I learnt the word *sharjay*- which meant hot and humid – and I would smile and mutter my new word miming exasperation at the heat to handfuls of middle aged male Baswari journalists. They would laugh (in confusion, pity, or friendship?). But when we took some group photographs with me at the centre only two of them stepped away for fear of reprisals from the photographic record. Although a fond memory, when I look at the image today of a grinning British woman amidst a group of Iraqi men, it somehow looks a bit pathetic. As if the photograph demonstrated my ability to sway Basrawi media towards balanced reporting! I wonder if they posed with their Iranian friends for photos too...

Another stark and somehow comic contrast sticks in my mind – the golf cart/warrior ratio. The moment saw me in a Foreign Office golf cart complete with Union flag painted on the roof, overflowing with BBC recording equipment, parked up on a dusty, scrubby road next to Saddam's Gate. The equipment is toppling, and Newsnight's Mark Urban is getting fidgety. The road is empty and he is looking at his watch and snuffling into his Arabic scarf. Camera woman Julie begins to unload the equipment onto the curb and Olivia (the only one in uniform) is nonchalantly chewing on a stalk of grass and gazing out across the waters of the Shatt. Mark excitedly shows me his camel bag – a gift from the military - basically a backpack full of water with a tube to drink from. Julie tries nervously to film the fisherman on the flowing waters. I told her to watch out for sniper fire, so she filmed from behind a T-wall. I perhaps should have taught them the jumpy vertical zig-zag manoeuvre but I think they would have found it out-of-line with their perception of me as a serious diplomat.

In a cloud of yellow dust and a roar of military might a convoy of tank-like Warrior vehicles start making their way towards us. They halt breathtakingly close and between us we begin to load the piles of black boxes into the back of one of the vehicles. It doesn't sound funny, but I did get the giggles. I found the golf cart/Warrior ratio quite symbolic of how the forces dwarfed the insubstantial civilian work in Iraq.

To add to the metaphor – I watched as Urban's dust-churning military convoy chopped through Saddam's Gate and into the city for a patrol. I ached to be able to go with them and swung the little golf cart back round towards the FCO compound. After a few metres the battery depleted and it took me twenty minutes to bring the cart a few hundred yards back to the office – first at a pathetic snail's pace and then ultimately by me getting out and pushing.

A short time later, our friendship grown, Olivia and I were none the luckier when we seconded another golf cart on an adventure to Uday's Palace. We whooped cheers at

Romanian soldiers as we hurtled past them on our commandeered vehicle. Olivia – even with her waist-length blond hair tied neatly in a military bun - was still a stunner. Our cheers weren't quite so audible on the return leg as we heaved the dead cart over a bridge past their compound. What a pair of idiots!

Olivia was key in helping me prepare for my biggest professional test in Basra – the arrival of Mr John Humphrys and the BBC Radio 4 Today team. We had to get the golf carts fully charged.

The Beeb

A few weeks before the decision was made for the programme to broadcast live from the Palace, a team of BBC researchers and producers had arrived to do a recce – to source interviewees and sites to use. Clearly the security situation deteriorated hugely in the short amount of time since their recce – and with hindsight we should never have given permission for the visit to go ahead. It took a huge amount of resource, at a fragile time during Britain's occupation and it endangered lives. I have to say that although the team on the ground approved it (including myself) we were driven to do so by Whitehall and by the increasingly futile *Better Basra* plan. I can only apologise to the Today team for making an ill-judged decision that bought them into the line of fire – but I also know that Mr Humphrys wouldn't have had it any other way.

My feet didn't touch the ground the week the team were in town – including the military escorts they numbered 12 in total. Our media massive was now a veritable platoon, as we were joined by the usual suspects, plus military media specialists and Whitehall press officers. I had no time for anything else and became a full time media baby-sitter/fixer.

Word of Humphrys' arrival in Iraq first reached me via the military rumour mill. We heard stories of his complaints about the lack of en-suite facilities at the Air Station before he even arrived at the Palace. We were filled with anxiety, but I reckoned I couldn't take the blame for the quality of his accommodation or lack of room service – that one must rest with his researchers. Praying for their safety started well before their helicopter landed at the Palace.

The team were to do two live broadcasts from the Palace, which included a certain amount of pre-recorded interviews and experiences, which they began capturing straight away. The FCO and the military bent over backwards to accommodate their every need – take them to a hospital, on patrol, to witness the *Better Basra* plan in action on the streets — but they still pushed for more and grumped as if we were somehow conspiring to keep news from them.

The first live broadcast went pretty well. They played some recorded material and we sat John next to the flowing Shatt Al-Arab in an office chair. He insisted on wearing his body armour and helmet throughout the broadcast — which I found amusing, as it was usually very difficult to get journalists to don their protection. Still, he looked good in the photos. I offered up the gently spoken Phil Jacobs who was Head Police Advisor to Basra Police, seconded from the South Wales Constabulary. He and John hit it off immediately and ended up in an unusually constructive conversation live on air. Phil came out with his classic line — *"look, this isn't Bangor it's Basra"* — which struck me as being a whole lot better and more honest than Kim Howells offering of *"it's starting to look like the sort of mess that most of us live in"*. We managed to get the military chaplain — known as the Padre - to do "Thought for The Day", but the BBC team were very jumpy (as was I) as we hadn't seen a draft of the Padre's words and had to rely on him to amble up to our broadcast point on time. Complete with walking staff, the Padre was a striking - if bizarre - figure and, as it turned out, eloquent enough.

What the team weren't made immediately aware of was that the night before the BBC's live broadcast from Saddam's Gate a mortar had landed within metres of the proposed site, making a dent in the road and sending shrapnel into our water tanks. It was a fantastic strategic hit if that was the intention - our precious clean water began spilling into the Shatt and the soldiers' ability to take showers was further reduced. We continued with the broadcast anyway, John Humphrys did notice the hole in the ground, but we shrugged it off in a "business-as-usual" kind of way.

With the first broadcast behind us we relaxed over breakfast and looked forward to tomorrow's show from the same spot, and an end to the hard work seemed almost in sight. The events of the rest of the day would change a lot of things.

It was the final day of Eid and despite our usual 24/7 working conditions, which meant it was impossible to observe any religious holiday at all, we were all given the day off work. I, of course, did not and could not oblige, but this time I was glad to have a ridiculously heavy workload and be safe in my office.

At about 2pm a Katyusha rocket slammed into the heart of the FCO compound. Several others followed. This time, it was too close and fast for some to run for cover and my journalist visitors, who had been sitting outside basking in the sunshine without their body-armour, literally hit the dirt. The shrapnel miraculously failed to penetrate a single person, but it tore through plastic chairs and took out a window 100m away. The BBC team were afraid, very afraid to be fair (apart from Jeremy - the quiet technician/producer who merely tucked a souvenir husk of shrapnel into his top pocket – I think he felt "lucky" at his narrow escape). Mark, one of the military media escorts was also caught outside at the time. Mark stands a swarthy six foot three at least, but somehow managed to fold himself up into a tight ball when he heard the first blast. He discovered when he uncurled himself that shrapnel holes in the wall and door around him were only millimetres from his head and body.

The decision was taken to move the broadcast spot the next morning to inside the PRT building. The BBC team needed no persuasion whatsoever to stay under hard cover and all of them were unusually conscientious about body armour and helmets.

The next morning, I got up before sunrise to let the BBC technician into the PRT building (missing my Tai Chi that morning). The only other person awake was Steve – a military escort with brilliant awareness of the role of the media (he was another bootneck too!) Steve and I were very diligent in our baby-sitting duties - military-savvy Paul Wood continued to wander off at every opportunity and was a frustration, but Humphrys needed to be kept intact – he was media royalty.

Amazingly, before I left my pod at 4am I penned a quick message to friends back home. They had all been alerted to the live BBC broadcasts and I was slightly concerned, particularly for my mum, that John's words that morning would cause unnecessary worry. I was also nervous about how the Today programme would cover the frightening events of the previous day. I wrote: *"I am not sure who heard the Today Programme on Monday "live from Basra Palace", but to reassure you, that we are not (not) living in a fortress under siege (well....ummm... not quite). But the US Apache helicopters have indeed arrived in town and are bursting onto our skyscapes (not sure whether this show of power makes me feel safer or not?) Anyway....whatever John says this morning....a pinch of salt....hmmm?"*

Almost as a way of reassuring my friends and family I also sent them a link to the following article. The piece is, of course, full of inaccuracies!

Whitehall staff enjoy swimming pool while squaddies sweat

Foreign Office bureaucrats are enjoying the delights of a swimming pool in one of Saddam Hussein's former Palaces, while British soldiers complain of water shortages and are being forced to use chemical toilets.

Troops in southern Iraq have revealed that the water purification plant at the Basra Palace complex is faulty. As a result, they say they do not have flushing toilets but even their portable chemical loos are not being cleaned out.

Soldiers say they have not received post for more than a week and no newspapers for two months. They add that the 'e-bluey' machine, which sends e-mails home, has been broken for several weeks.

By contrast, claim soldiers who have left messages on internet websites, 100 Foreign Office and other

Whitehall staff are living in luxury with a pool, en suite bathrooms, toilets and cable TV.

The Foreign Office claimed last night that the 30ft pool was available for use by military personnel. A spokesman said: "It's not one of the best places to be posted, so we make it as comfortable as possible."

But an Army source said: "We don't get time. We're too busy being bloody shot at. This kind of thing is terrible for morale."

A Ministry of Defence spokesman said last night: "They have the water supplies they need to operate in the difficult conditions, including showers. Mail is delivered daily."

He added that the chemical toilets were now being emptied after a contractor was replaced, and dismissed complaints about the lack of e-mail and newspapers.

Source: Christopher Lake, Mail on Sunday 15 October 2006

We all held our breath as Humphrys went live that morning. The BBC team had caught the sounds of the deafening explosion from the day before on tape and they opened the show with it.

Humphrys perhaps didn't know it, but this was the first time one of our reinforced hard-cover "pods" had received a direct hit. The pod in question belonged to Phil the South Wales Police Chief. Thankfully Phil was unhurt – his roof had a veritable hole in it – but it hadn't penetrated the pod fully. It was the ultimate test, but somehow as we swarmed to the site snapping pictures of the damage, we none of us felt reassured.

The sound of the explosion was broadcast, but with no real shift in narrative from the previous day. We sighed with

141

relief at the BBC's decision to report on some British successes as well as failures. Our enthusiasm won Steve and me a place in the hearts of the BBC team and not only was I allowed to listen and suggest edits on some of their pre-records, but we both appeared on the BBC website on Today's photographic journal of their visit. It was the busiest, and one of the most enjoyable weeks of my life and at one point, despite my cynicisms about an agenda-ridden BBC, I seriously considered a career in broadcast journalism. It wasn't that the content they produced was necessarily inspiring or life changing — it was the setting up, the production process and the whole "it's in the can" feeling that attracted me. It was in sharp contrast to my constant strategising and defensive press lines, which, by comparison, felt like a feeble and never-ending way of earning a living.

I'm sure some of my colleagues on camp resented my closeness to my media visitors and despite me explaining that journalists were only humans, many of them had a deep-rooted loathing of the profession. When I had the media in town I would stop being invited to social gatherings and the dining room would hush when I walked in with my guests. I was comfortable alongside them and felt able to speak freely (partly because I really believed my own press lines), but perhaps others saw it as just another unwelcome pressure of life at the Palace, having to watch what you said for fear it would be reported.

Perhaps the most moving and meaningful moment for me in Iraq was the time spent with John Humphrys and my Basrawi journalist friends as they explained what their lives were like under Saddam Hussein. John had allowed me to sit in, despite cynically suggesting that I had "set up" the journalists to be pro-British. Had he known me better, John would have known that I wouldn't have had the luxury, nor the inclination. We heard horrific stories of torture and mutilation, which the Today programme did an expert job of editing and broadcasting on the second day. It was something I had never heard them speak of before. We heard of nails being hammered into one man's back, tales of death, torture and intimidation. John was unusually quiet, certainly not his robust, argumentative self, and the group needed no prompting for words. When they had finished their tales, and John and I had thanked them for sharing, like a rather inadequate therapy session – the pair of us were paralysed in thought and we sat together in silence for many minutes.

"So, *it is all over now...maybe in more ways than one*", I wrote to friends later that day. John Humprys had said his final on-air goodbye from Basra and was back in his pod writing articles for the Mail and the Observer.

As he wrote, I did too. Our audiences were not so different and I was sure that my friends would be picking up The Observer at the weekend to see what John had to say. Here is what I wrote:

> *"I am at a point where I can say "it has been fun" as none of the interviews I set up were a complete disaster and nobody provided the BBC with any really negative sound bites. We have been working flat out doing everything from entertaining the Governor of Basra whilst he waited for John Humphrys, to organising the man's laundry (John not the Governor). At times I have felt like the landlady of a cheap hotel and at other times a spoilt media queen (calling up Press Office and demanding that the Foreign Secretary does a live interview, before realising her "foreign policy in Iraq is a disaster" gaff of yesterday). The Palace golf buggies have never seen so much action as I have been carting the BBC Defence Correspondent and radio equipment all over the place.*
>
> *Once everyone was packed up and ready for their departure by helicopter, Jason (aka Ambassador) and I took Jez the quietly spoken and ever so nice BBC technician on a tour of the compound (more golf cart abuse). Once you get beyond the tufty lawns of the*

FCO compound, beyond the Ghurkha gates and beyond again the military compound, past tired armoured personnel carriers and tired soldiers in their final few weeks here, you get to open space. Scrubland really, but after the claustrophobia of the compound it is great to see flowing channels of water and bird life – kingfishers and small bee eaters diving for insects and fish. The sandy ground gives a pinkish hue to the landscape and the odd reed and burst of green betrays the fact that the wonderful Shatt Al Arab is never far away. We were slightly more adventurous today and climbed inside the largest derelict Palace currently allocated to the UN (and therefore empty). [NB: This is Uday's Palace]. *The inlaid marble floors, delicately painted ceilings and wood carvings are nearly lost under a thick layer of dust embossed with military boot prints. Glass and wood splinters litter the place, but it is still breathtakingly beautiful and the view from the sandy stone balconies across the date palms and into Iran is inspiring.*

It is Eid in the Muslim world and Iraqi staff have bought in sweets for us. Mental note to self – must buy shed loads of chocolates for our Iraqi friends tomorrow. But Eid is not just about chocolate, it is about gun fire. Lots of it. A few nights ago the sky was lit up with tracer-fire as the people of Basra celebrated. I almost stopped to watch because it was so pretty before realising what goes up must come down. Still, it has prepared me for the fireworks night you are threatening me with. Think I will sit inside with my hands over my head if you don't mind. I may even weep (don't underestimate my nervous condition).

Janet – my god, you don't email much, but when you do you set the keyboard on fire! Too many questions! Too many questions! Erm...some answers to some of them.

144

1) *Yes, General Sir Richard Dannatt has indeed set the cat among the pigeons somewhat – I expect you are all sick to death with news on this bloody country by now. I think that's the plan actually – get the British public so fed up with hearing about Iraq you won't notice/care when a real decision about what we actually do here is made.*

2) *"Is there any good stuff you can tell us about?" Yes loads, that is what I do for a living – 800km of water pipes laid, electricity supplied to 85,000 homes last month, 50 tons of books given to the University, we have re-flooded the marshes back up to 67% (drained by Saddam down to 6% destroying livelihoods)...shall I go on?*

3) *"Is there a free local press?" Yes and no. Far more so than under Saddam. They tend to report flat facts only however (which isn't bad, just lacks style). Some are prepared to report the British side, but many get threatened by the militia (not naming names but the Al Mahdi Army mainly). Main problem I have is with Al Alam (Iranian) who blatantly pump inaccurate anti-British news into Basra.*

That's all for now, dears. Until we meet in dear old England. Make sure it is cold and raining for me please.

Eid Mubarak

xxxxxxxxxxxxxxxxxxxxxxxxxxxxxxxxxxxxxxx

But despite my planned R&R break in the UK and intention to return to Basra, the above message was my very last message sent from the Palace – the next time I was to write to my friends would be from Kuwait.

I wasn't cracking under pressure – but our mission felt like it was. There was one man, however, who thought that I had lost it — our Deputy Head of Mission and de facto Head of Security. Chris the KBR manager was away and I was staying in his pod as mine was overflowing with journalists. Although he was a smoker, Chris didn't like smoke in his room — so late one night I clunked open his door and stood one step outside in the night time air to enjoy some nicotine. I was of course "breaking the rules" — by loitering outside — and of course I had no body armour on. I had forgotten (or didn't care) that James, the sweet and terribly old-fashioned security manager lived next door to Chris — and it placed James in a very difficult position when he swung open his door to catch me in the act. He had to report me to the Head of Security.

This one member of the British Foreign Service was quite well known for his sternness. My ambition had been to ensure that every exchange I had with him evoked at least a brief smile to curb his usual sneer. I had no chance for smiles this time. Several days after the cigarette crime, on the same day as an incoming rocket had nearly killed John Humphrys (and with very little sleep to support me), the man tore into me for my outrageous abuse of the rules - the outdoor midnight fag. I felt tears stinging my eyes. Exhausted from the BBC visit - he was the only man to make me cry in a number of years. Although I will not forgive him for that, somewhere inside I do understand the pressure he was under to reign in potentially life-threatening behaviour. But sadly his perception was that crying was a sign of weakness. As John Gray quite rightly put it, "a woman under stress is not immediately concerned with finding solutions to her problems but rather seeks relief by expressing herself and being understood." If only he had grasped this, he might have earned more respect of his female colleagues and not have told me to shape up or ship out.

So before I did shape up and ship out (which had nothing at all to do with my smoking gaffe and consequent tears), I had the presence of mind to make this final entry into my diary, as I packed my bags to leave. It speaks for itself.

There was a lot that I couldn't explain to my dear friends by email, as I know they would fear my safety. Quite aside from the excitement of the bloody BBC being here all week, things have started to get very hairy. The attacks against the British bases in Basra have increased. October has been the worst month this year, we are up to 85 rocket or mortar attacks and the month has not even ended. Usually they come at night, but the number of missiles per attack has upped from the usual one or two to as many as 20 in one go — we think they must have a multiple rocket launcher.

We had a close run thing last Friday as everyone on the compound was enjoying some outside time at a hastily organised barbecue. Animal flesh, sausages and chicken wings were scattered widely as a mortar landed within yards, sending people frantically running for cover. Although terrifying (if in another slightly Carry-on moment), thankfully nobody was injured. Despite my vegetarian ways, I was on my way to enjoy a rare moment of barbecued socialising and only about 100 yards away when the mortar struck forcing me to hammer on the door of the nearest inhabited pod to provide me with cover. I am not sure that Aussie David was too thrilled by my company for the following hour of lock down, but what could you do? At least we had the bloody "strategy" to talk about!

And then came the Today Programme. All in all the show was fair and balanced in their reporting and as the Consul General said "we got our key messages out" (the strategy beginning to take hold at last). No 10 are apparently "not happy" with it, but my God it could have been much worse had any one of the interviewees gaffed a negative slant or heaven forbid, if the lovely Humphrys or his entourage been taken out by enemy fire.

In London, Downing Street are apparently, as I write this, considering our future here. (Should we stay or should we go....if we stay there could be trouble......if we go.....you know the rest). It is heart breaking. All the civilians here in the compound believe they can make a difference to Basra, if only the militia would let us. This past week I met with some of the Basrawi Police to talk about how to equip their media team – I really want to help them. Every single Iraqi I have met is utterly charming (with the possible exception of Governor Wai'li who has no eye contact and a poor aura).

Here we are us Brits – still trying desperately with our "hearts and minds" approach under heavy bombardment, because even those who aren't tree hugging hippies like me, know it is the right way. Aside from the attempts on my life (as I said a female diplomat would score well amongst my attackers) – I am also up against Iranian propaganda machines who are bent on removing us from Iraq and painting us as villains. Rather than block Iranian TV channels (which some think would be a good idea), I wish I had the chance to sit down and talk with people like Al Alam and those who control it and explain our good intentions. Perhaps they could explain theirs.....what do they want? A Shiastan in the south? To control Basra's oil? Does it really boil down to cold hard cash and territorial control? It is an age old struggle I guess, but I am longing for humanity to wake up and listen to their "hearts and minds" and know, really know, that being constantly driven by a control of money and land doesn't lead to happiness for anyone.

What strikes me about this diary entry was that despite having been under daily assault for close to a hundred days, there was still a naïve idea that my attackers could be sat down and talked out of it. There was still an assumption that by appealing to people's better side they would give up age-old habits of fighting over territory and material gain.

Looking back, I was clearly exhausted. Not wanting to let go, my wits were at an end as the security situation slowly prised the notion of a British-made *Better Basra* out of my grasp. In reality the task was nigh impossible – there was a dire lack of human resources, a lack of ability to operate effectively under fire, and a lack of strategic direction - miraculous given that the British had been in Basra for over three years already. Those against us were not simply hitting us with bombs – the weapons of mass persuasion were in full use. Here is a taste of that in the form of a direct transcript from Al Alam (TV) on the reaction from the people of Basra to call for British troops to pullout:

> *[Television correspondent Nu'aymah Abd-al-Razzaq] - Assuming direct responsibility for the deterioration of the situation in southern Iraq and the demand for a swift withdrawal of the British forces in order to curb the exacerbation of crises which it caused since it occupied Iraqi soil. These statements which were made by the head of the British army are received with identical reactions in Basra. The reactions were unanimous on the need to translate such statements into a practical move and to effectively announce the date for the withdrawal of the British forces from southern Iraq.*

> *[Unidentified Iraqi] The British are the cause of the psychological worry. They are the cause of the political, social and development problems in the Basra Governorate. If they withdraw, as they did in Al-Amarah City, I am sure that well-being will reign in the entire governorate.*

> *[Nu'aymah] Some observers argue that the growing opposition by the population, the increase in missile attacks which target the headquarters of the British forces in Basra and the increase in the number of victims, in addition to the swelling of casualties in the ranks of the British soldiers, may be the main reason which led the head of the British army to admit the*

failure of his forces in achieving anything positive in southern Iraq, in particular, and in the region in general.

[Unidentified Iraqi] They have caused problems to the Basra population, particularly through raids, arrests and the destruction of the infrastructure.

[Another unidentified Iraqi] Basra now is witnessing an intensive development campaign. Then the British forces come and sabotage this development. Thus they are not wanted by the Basra population.

[Another unidentified Iraqi] They are the cause of crises, of the political and security problems and of the violations which happened in Basra.

The very notion that it was (effectively) being put about that the British were sabotaging development in Basra made my blood boil at the time. If this was true, then this was certainly not known by staff at the High Commission compound. Perhaps the stories that were being floated about that the Al Mahdi Army were screwing plaques claiming credit for the construction of coalition-funded schools and clinics was propaganda too – but I am not so sure.

In the weeks and days before I left Basra the tone of my emails to friends and family got more and more exasperated. I complained to them that the British public were disconnected with Iraq and when my brother wrote to say that there was *"too much rhetoric on Iraq going on"* it was met with an angry retort, *"there may be rhetoric here, but there are also people dying and real things being done!"* I should have known better. Exclamation marks didn't serve to emphasise the point, instead they conveyed my frustration – but my sentences continued to end with them. Still as John wrote his newspaper stories in his room, I continued to pound the keyboard in mine:

150

*I disagree with Humphrys that money is needed here!
There is plenty of money in Iraq (take the $170m held
in Baghdad destined for Basra) - what Basra needs
isn't money, it is management. Management of
people, management of money, management of
expectations. In fact all these elements are very much
needed on this compound too!!!*

(you see the exclamation mark fatigue)

*To borrow Mark Etherington's phrase - who said this
line many times when I pushed him at journalists, the
convincing speaker he is – "I remain a stubborn
optimist". Despite the increasing onslaught of militia
attacks and the intimidation of the good people of
Basra - I have a perhaps naïve hope and belief that
Basra will work out in the end. It has to. It has a
port, fertile land, and bags of oil. Its precarious
geographical position between Saudi, Kuwait and
Iran are perhaps what is holding it all back. One
thing is for sure, without the support of those three
countries it may not realise its full potential.*

I stopped writing eventually. A few hours later we were
finally waving off the BBC Today team, grinning our
goodbyes through gritted teeth. After over a week of intense
work and journalist-sitting, Jason and I were close to
collapse. As mentioned, we had given up our pods so that
the team could be more comfortable and we were very glad to
be back in our own spaces. Jason had been sharing with the
BBC Iraqi translator, Mohammed, who was badly shaken up
by the rocket which narrowly missed the team. The
explosion was right next to Jason's pod and Mohammed had
been inside it taking a rest at the time. Many reassurances
had to be made and Mohammed claimed Basra Palace was
the most dangerous place he had ever been to in Iraq. Paul
Wood had kindly filled my fridge with chocolate when he left,
by way of thanks. I realised I hadn't managed a Tai Chi
session for over a week and could really tell the difference.
As we watched the helicopter shudder away into the Iraq

night, we decided then and there to give ourselves a well-earned day off work the following day.

Escape From Disaster

Foreign Secretary Margaret Beckett today admitted historians could judge Iraq as a foreign policy disaster for Britain.

Source: London Evening Standard, 23 October 2006

Last week, Prime Minister Tony Blair was asked whether the violence in Iraq had "so far been pretty much of a disaster".

He replied: "It has."

But Downing Street later said the prime minister's words had been misinterpreted.

Reported [nevertheless] by the BBC November 2006

The following day began with the luxury of a barefoot Tai Chi exercise next to the lake. Luckily the lake had recently been cleared of the floating corpses of fish caused by IDF hitting their waters. The cat that usually joined me as a charming distraction was missing, but some early morning joggers nodded their hellos in the pink early morning light as I gazed ahead of me and focussed on my ten-minute short martial form. Slipping into my sandals when I finished, I headed for the cook-house for my breakfast of a single boiled egg. The day was feeling pure and uncluttered already, and notably free of house-guests to look after. As with most "days off work", after breakfast I checked into the office to respond to a flurry of emails from London (they wanted debriefing following the departure of John H & co.) It wasn't until Jason called me later in the morning saying "Oi, Baroness, you are not supposed to be working", did I drag myself away. We spent a fun couple of hours, swimming, sun bathing and playing a complicated pool game of "rockets of mortars" which we invented using old water bottles. We stacked them up next to the pool and bobbed about laughing in the water throwing either a "mortar" (filled water bottle which went high and came down on top of the stack) or a "rocket" (far more fun to throw, fast and hard, smashing the piled water bottles from the side). We even engaged the services of an advisor from the North Wales police, who was our official stacker upper.

Next we "borrowed" two of the much acclaimed golf carts and set off around the Palace. There was one incoming attack alarm, which caught us without body armour in the military cook-house off the FCO compound, but it was a false one – and unusually no explosions were forthcoming. Nevertheless we headed back to home territory - the batteries were running flat on the carts anyway and, try as we might, they failed to take air over bumps. We decided to go for a long walk around the largest of the lakes, and sat side by side throwing pebbles in the water and watching the colourful birds darting for their prey. If we did not feel like brother and sister by this stage (our parents, the Foreign Office) it might have been romantic. We spoke about how calm and quiet it was, how relieved we were that our guests had left and what work there was to do next. I remember saying that I felt everything was about to change, but I had no idea that we would be packing to leave that night.

Not more than an hour later, Jason was caught outside during our biggest attack yet. He survived intact, but I can only imagine what the sound of 22 rockets landing in close proximity was like. Miraculously no one was killed, but several people were badly injured, doors were blown off buildings on the army side, and vehicles written-off. Jason made his decision then and there. He was un-volunteering for this assignment. He called to tell me about it and I immediately convened a meeting in my pod (I had lots of chocolate). Jason was quite right. The situation WAS dangerous. We didn't need No. 10 to decide that from two thousand six hundred miles away. It was just a matter of time before one of us got unlucky. We had many close shaves. We had experienced the death of one civilian, poor Julio – and the continual news of military fatalities were felt keenly. Rockets were beginning to land more often and with more accuracy – tearing through accommodation blocks, offices and social facilities. In addition to this, we were unable to do our jobs properly. We lacked sleep. We lacked resources. We couldn't get out into Basra City - EVERY application I had sent to our security managers had been denied – I was a target. It was a nonsense to have a media team who had no on-the-ground experience of Basra.

The Consul General, Rosalind Marsden, was contacted and she managed to slip over to my pod after the all clear had been given. She sat in my room with her armed guard perilously waiting for her outside as Jason and I told her that we were both un-volunteering. I was a mother of three, after all. I really didn't want to leave my kids without a mother, and perhaps I would be doing more good being with them now, than I would be helping the people of Basra - something I didn't seem to have been able to excel at. We spoke for a long time. We spoke frankly about our work and the restrictions upon us, most of which The Consul General was aware of anyway. When she left she told us not to speak to anyone for the moment, she had some calls to make. Our departure could potentially, be part of a wider evacuation of more staff, rather than an "un-volunteering".

We booked ourselves onto the outgoing helicopter that night and I dashed to the office to close up shop with a lump in my throat. Spinning out a ton of explanatory emails that afternoon, the most difficult were to the many Iraqi journalists I had convinced of my own personal commitment to supporting them. I felt like a sham. Despite my carefully constructed press lines, I was cutting and running – shaping up and shipping out.

Emails done, before I headed for the pub for a stiff drink, I wrote some slightly sarcastic final words in my diary:

> *I sense something big is to come....death, life, love, enlightenment, who knows, but I am busy packing up my essential possessions (sketch pad and moisturiser) and tonight we will board a Merlin out of here. Whether I ever return remains to be seen, but I hope*

if/when we all pull out of Uday's former Palace (an uncomfortable location if you ask me — too many ghosts) and the locals loot the place, I hope that someone nice gets my IKEA rugs, candles and colourful posters of Asian spice markets. May Peace Be Upon Them.

In the bar the crowds had gathered as much to find out what was happening as to wish Jason and I well. Military friends patted me on the shoulder in unusual shows of affection, and far too many people said that this was no place for a woman and that I should go back to my children. Jason appeared nervous and still shaken by his earlier experience (he was twitchy and on edge at every door slam). The sandwich thief looked like another candidate for un-volunteering as he had not only taken to wearing body armour and helmet indoors under hard cover — but he had also bought ballistic sunglasses and now never took them off. People wrote messages of support and email addresses in my sketch book and even the toughest among us admitted to being afraid of late. When the Consul General arrived to say goodbye and buy me a drink (of alcohol) she gave me the news that London had ordered the first stage of evacuation for the civilians at the Palace. I was not an un-volunteer, I was an evacuee.

On arrival in Kuwait I was to help support the management of the evacuation of up to 30 staff initially. The Telegraph journalist was looming unaccompanied on the compound, press statements needed to be prepared, and with a two day journey to Kuwait via Baghdad, I still had plenty of work ahead of me.

Strawberries & Cream

Dairy entry, 1 November 2006 from Kuwait

There is no need to email the girls back home anymore, I have texted them all and spoken on the phone to Louise. We fly back home tomorrow and will land in Bourn village to a welcome of cheap chardonnay and probably much relief.

This is being written from my apartment in Kuwait. The kids are running around as if nothing has happened, as if I have never been away. They ask me for a drink and the little one tells tales that his older brother has been hitting him and asks for help to get him onto the next level of his Playstation game (a skill I have cunningly avoided). My nearly teenage daughter grumpily lolls around my neck in a way that says she missed me, but she is far too cool to express it too much.

The journey back to the safety of my Kuwait City apartment was every bit as bizarre and exhilarating as the road trip across the Kuwait-Iraq border back in July. I made it onto the Merlin with only a two hour wait in the darkness at the helipad at Basra Palace. Anything that was dear to me was stuffed into the backpack strapped to my back on top of body armour and the talk amongst the soldiers as they waited with me was of one thing — the increase in attacks, how dangerous it had become. Earlier in the day, more blasts could be heard across the compound as a rocket exploded right outside the military Head Quarters, and another destroyed three vehicles on the American part of the compound. It was strangely reassuring to learn that the soldiers too had sleepless nights and startled when doors banged - us civilians were not merely cissies that couldn't hack it — our fear was legitimate. But standing in the night waiting for the chug of the helicopter hidden by the darkness there was a clear sense of abandoning ship, of being a quitter. I vowed then to find a way to continue to help the people of Basra; particularly those brave and dedicated journalists whom I had got to know and made what felt like empty promises to in the early days.

The chopper arrived amid a swirl of grit and sand and I made my final run across the now familiar battle-worn patch of concrete. I no longer felt like Private Benjamin – instead a fully paid up cast-member in a war-movie with a solemn end. Tears stung my eyes as we lunged away in the great metal flying machine and there was no sense of the relief usually felt on landing at Basra Air Station. CRG security staff showed me my room for the night (or the few hours left of night that remained). They expected me to be delighted with the double bed and TV in the room; instead I just looked up to the tin ceiling and shook my head. No it wasn't "hard cover" and despite being shown where the nearest bunker was, I slept fitfully on top of the bed with my body armour on.

A group of five of us booked onto the Hercules flight bound for Kuwait (via Baghdad) the next morning: myself; Jason; Etta (a DFID colleague), David and Ole. Ole was a Danish agricultural expert who had worked in Iraq for the previous three years helping to increase tomato and wheat production and very much involved in the successful re-flooding of the Arab marshlands. He was nick-named "Granddad" because of his gentleness, his greying beard and his wealth of experience. His departure was somehow symbolic.

But perhaps more symbolic for me personally was how I coped with the flight ahead of me. A nervous flyer on commercial flights, I was really dreading the webbing seats and cramped conditions in the back of the Hercules. I shuffled on, at least there wasn't the sense of urgency that boarding a helicopter brings as it touches down for a just a matter of minutes. The Herc was on the tarmac for quite a while. We were told quite aggressively by the Loadmaster to take no photographs. Perhaps his attitude was because I had found John Humphrys' Press pass left in his room and attached it to my body armour as a perverse souvenir. I clipped the pass off my body armour and dropped it into the pouch that hung around my neck. Pulling out my sketchbook, I set about drawing the interior of the plane to distract me from my flight nerves. I was quietly quite terrified at the prospect of being air-borne in this tatty looking plane. During the 20 minute delay the Loadmaster spotted me and suggested a trip to the flight deck to sketch the pilots. Before I knew it, myself and a very bouncy and excited Etta, were up in the cockpit chatting and laughing with the two men responsible for flying the plane. We were given headsets to communicate with them, listen to air traffic control, and to hear some bad 80's tracks from one of the pilot's iPods. We were given fresh strawberries (which seemed somehow strange), and Etta and I marvelled at the chatty casualness of the pilots.

Having learned to enjoy helicopter flights, my fear of plane travel remained. However, when the pilots told us to stand up behind them as we came into land, I discovered the most remarkable way to banish the phobia. In an extreme tactical landing into Baghdad, the mighty plane tore almost vertically, head-first through the clouds – with the pilots whopping for joy. As a result of this awesome adrenalin rush, quite uncharacteristically, I couldn't wait to board the plane again for the Baghdad- Kuwait leg of the journey.

My experiences were clearly changing me. "Welcome back to being ugly," announced one of the Hercules pilots as we landed in Kuwait. Grinning at him, I realised that whilst my self-esteem may have been artificially raised, I too had toughened up and was brimming with confidence despite his remark. Confidence that would be confused with aggression by those close to me, and even I was surprised at how obedient my own children were when I prepared them for their school day with military precision and a new-found authority.

If someone had told me that at the age of 36 I would be flying in a military aircraft into Baghdad I would have laughed. There was a new feeling that I was capable of pushing myself far further than ever imagined, both physically and mentally. Next to the sketch of the pilots I wrote, *"there is no doubt that this experience has made me stronger and that my life is only just beginning".*

By the time I got to Kuwait, others from the compound had begun to evacuate and Thomas Harding from the Telegraph (who had been lurking) had got hold of the evacuation story. Rosalind, the Consul General was furious, as she said, quite rightly it gave the impression that the militia were winning and it seriously endangered the lives of those left behind (when it became known that the British were beginning to pull out of Camp Abu Naji the attacks became ferocious). On arrival in Kuwait I immediately began helping with the evacuation and Press Statements from both Rosalind and the Foreign Secretary.

Beckett was quoted on the BBC website as saying, *"British soldiers and civilians are working in tough conditions and with considerable courage.....but as I have said to this House before, we owe it to our own forces and to the Iraqi people to hold our nerve in this critical period."* My nerve had not held and I couldn't help recalling Beckett's own worthless trip to Basra. This was a political game. On the same day the BBC also reported that Liberal Democrat leader Sir Menzies Campbell had said: *"Mrs Beckett's comments are notable as much for what she doesn't say as for what she does".*

9/11

By the ninth of November 2006, I was once more standing in the school playground in my desert boots. My marriage on the rocks, but my children once more running into my arms. And although tired and confused, restless and slightly jumpy – I was thoroughly happy to be alive. There was, however a part of me still in Basra with the few staff that remained and with the people and friends of Basra city.

In England I set about writing some final thoughts. But it was still too close to be able to see the longer term effects that Basra had on me. The need to write was, and remains to this day, a form of therapy for me – but it is hoped that by sharing all that happened during my 100 days in Iraq, that it will be far more than an intriguing story for my grandchildren. I hope that by understanding some of my feelings and behaviour it will better prepare others who in a moment of bravery, naivety or down right what-the-fuck-ery volunteer for such an assignment.:

> *How am I left with feeling about my experience? It was hoped this would be a humorous tale of a middle class housewife trying to make good of Basra, but I fear it has turned into a rather depressing account which has had a tendency to slip into semi-political ranting. I guess there is only so far you can take the interior décor of your pod and weekend shopping at the Naafi when you are in a war zone - although it should be noted, I did manage to pick up an Iraqi flag and a pack of the CIA's 'most wanted' playing cards.*
>
> *Working with the media has been a real eye opener. I have met just a few international journalists so it may be unfair of me to judge, but there are some obvious contrasts. When thinking of CNN's Michael Ware – a fierce Australian entrenched in Baghdad for the past few years - he had a real thirst for information and lusted after truth and understanding. He was battle*

weary and tough and spoke of burning bodies littering the streets where he lived, but he challenged our work with passion and real experience. Perhaps I am naïve (I have said this more than once), but Michael seems to be what journalism should be about, and like him or not, you have to respect him for the passion in his craft.

The comparison with the BBC team and with John Humphrys in particular offers a disturbing contrast. John's article in the Observer made me very cross when I read it. My mind cast back to his last afternoon in Basra (and my pen-ultimate) when we were both locked away writing in our pods. Me writing my diary, him writing newspaper stories. When the rocket hit Phil's pod, I specifically asked the BBC not to broadcast news of the impact point. It was the first FCO pod to be directly hit. It is basic common sense security, the militia would know where to fire at again if they learn of their success. So you can imagine how delighted I was to see not only details, but photographs of the impact point in Humphrys' Observer article. Perhaps he thought that saying the rocket hit the roof of his producers pod (a huge distortion of the truth) made it ok.

As charming as he was to me, John appears to be just a celebrity broadcaster who wanted to add Iraq to his CV before his retirement date. And I wasn't the only person to say so – some of his own research team planted that thought in my mind.

The BBC team lacked Michael Ware's thirst for the truth – from the outset they had formed an opinion, an agenda, despite their lack of inquiry. Paul Wood was perhaps the only one with a glimmer of understanding, but he too appeared to have pretty much made up his mind on the flavour of his reporting and was merely gathering evidence to support his already formed theories.

162

My god. Enough ranting about the BBC already. Let me remember my top good moments in Basra, the "rays of sunshine" as Phil, my police colleague would say.

1) **Dates stuffed with walnuts**, *a gift from journalist Mahmood - and scoffing a whole tray-full in less than an hour – Philippa and I were left with sticky fingers and sore tummies – but they were delicious. I have never eaten dates before and they were wonderful, as was the invite from Abdul, another journalist to eat dates from his garden. In years to come I will do just that, Abdul, Inshallah.*

2) **Views.** *Dripping with sweat and climbing high inside the ruins of the Hussein Palaces, Saddam's Gates or to the top of Ghurkha positions just for a chance to glimpse a far-reaching view of the outside world. Seeing what remained of date palm plantations - chopped down by Saddam during the Iran-Iraq war - the flowing Shatt, the small fishing boats casting their nets, the city. Deprived of any form of a "view" behind concrete bomb blast "T walls", when an effort was made to see the bigger picture, it never failed to overwhelm.*

3) **Laughing.** *I had my moments when the tears rolled from laughter. One that stands out was when my office mate, Jawwad and I drafted ideas for my cartoon on how to escape the compound. The cartoon was an artists' backlash against the many rules we have to adhere to and recommended hording coat hangers, flushing tampons down the toilets and stealing guns from CRG as examples. Another moment of mirth involved the wide eyed security manager James and a fabricated press leak. He was very, very worried. We laughed a lot – even the mean spirited Deputy.*

4) **The joy of seeing children**. *It rarely happened and when I did see a kid, I missed my own so much I almost wished I hadn't. From the Ghurkha Sanger position I saw female tots on the*

163

ground with scruffy ponytails picking through the rubble and rubbish to be at the side of a female relative. The boys though, whilst just like my own – tenacious and cheeky, leapt across the rooftops almost at eye level, viewed through the netting on the Sanger from where I peeped.

5) *Finally I would also add **seeing people at their very best** – brave and committed. I know it is speech writing stuff, but it is genuinely meant.*

Perhaps I should have done this the other way around, but here is the top four of worst things about Basra:

1) ***Panic.** Worse than a mortar or rocket landing – which, although loud and scary, it is over pretty quickly - is the panic you feel for others. When the rocket hit the accommodation block during the BBC visit we first heard (incorrectly) that it had hit the KBR manager's pod. Dave sometimes worked from his pod and we spent a good ten minutes not being able to remember when we last saw him. We even started talking about Dave in the past tense! (He was fine). The worst, of course, was getting Saman's phone call after the rocket went through his accommodation. I can't explain how it feels to know someone is hurt and not be able to go to them.*

2) ***Knowing the BBC had recorded a very loud explosion and my friends and family were listening back home.***

3) ***Getting to know my bathroom.** Perhaps they reinforce bathrooms more for those who are likely to pooh their pants in fear. I got to know that small room very well!*

4) *The ultimate **disappointment** – not doing enough for the people of Basra and having to leave before I had really "made a difference".*

It is the good memories that will be savoured for much longer. The girls in Bourn, and my other friends and family have kept me strong by emailing me about their own lives. I still have goodness in my heart and a glimmer of determination.

Where I go from here is anyone's guess. I know what I would like to do. I would like to find a large attic room in the west country, with some views of green pastures dusted in drizzle with a smattering of cows. Some huge canvasses to paint and a laptop, overflowing ashtrays and a few bottles of red wine. Coffee stains on wooden floor boards and a big hairy dog dozing in the corner. Paint brushes, pens, paint splatters and the phone off the hook. And after I have got all that out of my system....I may think about a posting to Baghdad.

Assaf

Well, the story did - and will forever - continue. Once settled back in England I briefly joined the Iraq Operations Team at the FCO and helped with the eventual closure of the whole Palace base and relocation of the Embassy Office to the Air Station (renamed the Central Operating Base or COB).

One real pleasure was to help with a visit from Basra's Judiciary – including the female judge I encountered in Iraq. She was accompanied by a group of police, lawyers and judges and of course the charming, and clever Assaf. As I previously mentioned, Assaf worked closely with the female judge, spoke excellent English and was a huge support in facilitating meetings between the Provincial Reconstruction Team and the Basra Judiciary. I had always been impressed with his commitment to building a "better Basra" and was delighted to see him again, and in such good spirits.

The group visited the Surrey police and met British judges, lawyers and police. I helped with the media, and they found themselves in national newspapers (bizarrely talking about parking tickets) and giving radio interviews. A very amusing evening was spent at the hotel with Assaf – he had sent me lots of hilarious YouTube clips of Iraqi Sheiks dancing and we spent most of the night huddled over his mobile phone laughing. Younger than me, Assaf had a baby son and a wife back in Iraq. He was optimistic and stubborn (as was Etherington) about Basra's future and I felt heartened that such a clever, funny, charismatic man would return to help Basra on its way, where I couldn't. Assaf mentioned, not for the first time that he had received threats, but he shrugged off suggestions - made by me and some of his concerned British police friends - that he should consider an asylum application. Such was his commitment.

Sadly, back in Iraq, a short time later Assaf was shot dead by an assassin on a motorcycle. His death rocked me more than any of my own near-death explosions. More than any anonymous mortar-fire or silly rocket blinds. More than helicopter shoot downs or roadside bombs. Assaf was shot in the head at close range and was singled out, specifically targeted. It was personal and painful. Assaf represented all the hope I had left behind. Unable to directly impact the reconstruction of Iraq, I at least felt that this young man — a brave, intelligent Iraqi man, represented the real potential that this amazing nation held. I dared to think the word "hope" when I thought of Assaf.

When I learned of his death — standing in my father's Oxfordshire kitchen — I felt further away from Iraq than ever. Somehow Assaf's murder felt like my own failure. And I wept properly for the first time since I left. My dream of a *Better Basra* finally shattered.

My father tried to comfort me and let me know that there was something on the FCO website about the "strategic withdrawal of FCO staff from Basra Palace". I told him that I wasn't going back and hinted perhaps that the words on the website (which may well have been penned by my own hand) could be taken with a pinch of salt. My dad remembers to this day that I informed him I had been evacuated from Basra 'under a hail of rocket and machine-gun fire'. If you look at the photos we took as we pulled funny faces in sand-bagged bunkers, or the fooling around in body armour at the pool - you may be forgiven for thinking this statement was my Hilary Clinton in Bosnia moment. But, what I wanted to express to a man whom I loved and respected, was the contrast between the offered public line and the reality. Hopefully this piece of writing does that. And explains to my father, quite why Assaf's death meant so much to me.

Epilogue

The Palace (and eventually the whole of the country) was handed over to the Iraqis, and apparently it is to become a museum (not a health spa). We still have a presence in Basra, but the majority of troops are now entrenched in another battle for hearts and minds in Afghanistan.

I never quite made it to the romantic attic, overlooking countryside. Never got a dog, I even gave up smoking – and I never liked coffee anyway. Peter and I split up fairly soon after my arrival back, and he shares his life with someone new not 20 miles away. The kids live with me and are a continual joy – even if my eldest son does seem to have an unusual attraction to danger.

In 2009 I married James, who has never been to war, or on a diplomatic assignment, nor even a secret mission. We met on the internet and courted via the written word. He is someone who seems to be able to understand and support me entirely, perhaps because he has spent most of his adult life living outside of Britain, or perhaps because he is quite simply my soul mate.

James watched me paint a series of portraits largely inspired by my time in Iraq (and including the face of none other than John Humphrys). On my birthday in 2009, we both welcomed guests at the opening of my exhibition of the portraits at The Frontline Club in London. It was wonderful to be able to introduce James to some of my friends I served with in Basra who were able to attend.

In 2007, I was awarded a medal for my efforts in reconstructing Iraq, which made my mum and dad very proud, I'm sure. However, I was one of hundreds who received it. Some of the medals were sent in the mail in jiffy bags – which defeated the object of making our contributions feel treasured, I fear.

As of July 2011, I still haven't made it back to Basra (watch this space), but last year, in a break away from the FCO, I spent a week in Baghdad under a contract for Dieter's company (Albany Associates). I was training the press team from the Iraqi Ministry of Human Rights – teaching them all I knew about building a communications strategy. Jawwad also made it to Baghdad – for a whole new posting, as Press & Public Affairs Officer at the British Embassy! He has only just returned – and remains a picture of calm to this day.

Jason continued a career in communications but left the FCO soon after we returned and after a year working for Dieter in Sudan, he moved to Dubai. Philippa and a number of others have also left public service. The Deputy was awarded an MBE for his exceptional service in Iraq (a-hem) and the young, laid-back Chris was last seen working in the office of the Prime Minister.

I still keep in contact with some of the international and Basrawi journalists I met during my time there, and the girls in Bourn village continue to be a force for good. Although I no longer live there, I catch up with some of them from time to time. My decision to spend time in Afghanistan a year or so after my return from Iraq wasn't popular with all of them.

Although I insist that my experience was one of Post Traumatic *Development,* rather than *Stress Disorder* – the ghosts of Basra remain. I don't start at doors banging any more or fireworks, but stress and difficult experiences can provoke a return of disturbing dreams set amongst the rubble of Iraqi homes. Hyper-vigilance and "control cleaning" are also behaviours new to me since being in Iraq.

My own personal Iraq story is mainly a positive one. I learned that I was strong and capable. I also learned that I could be weak and vulnerable. I learned that being a woman (particularly a mother) in a military environment could be a great asset. And I ultimately learned that actually, you can make a difference – even if it is just to one person for one minute. As for a civvy not belonging in a war film? Well maybe not a brainless action movie, but no post-war effort would work without them.

170

I escaped disaster in Iraq, but tragedy struck very close to home a few years later, when my mother was killed in a car accident. This personal experience of crippling loss and despair brought home to me the depth and breadth of suffering in somewhere like Iraq – death of a loved one can *never* become everyday or common-place, no matter how often it happens. It will always be life-changing, perception-shifting, all consuming and destroying. Not surprisingly, when my mother died, some of my stress behaviours returned. Again, I share this because I am keen that people are prepared both pre and post deployment to a conflict area. The shadows of trauma can remain and can be triggered years after the experience. The loss of my mum, perhaps with my Iraq experiences catching up with me, forced me to focus on what I wanted from my one, unique time on this planet.

Perhaps it was also revisiting Iraq via John Chilcott's Inquiry, together with a continual disillusionment about my ability to make a difference with the Foreign Office (I had been struggling with another frustrating role as Head of Communication for Pakistan) lead me to a big decision.

In October 2011 I applied for, and was successfully awarded early severance. I wasted no time in enrolling in a full time Masters in Fine Arts. A whole new career and life awaits.

Once more I'd like to thank Sir John Chilcot and his team (particularly Baroness Usha Prashar) for their warm encouragement for us to share our stories and for reigniting the desire to share my own story beyond my family.

> *"I wish I was there with you. I'm sorry I can't be. But to you and everybody else on operations at the moment, we would like to say 'stay safe'"* - Prince William. To fellow British soldiers in Iraq. The Prince was due to be deployed in Basra, in Iraq, in 2007, but military commanders decided it was too much of a risk.

PHOTOS

Top; With a group of Basrawi journalists October 2006;
Bottom: That photo from the forklift.

Top: with HM Ambassador to Baghdad Dominic Asquith;
Bottom: With BBC's Mark Urban

174

Top: Warning stay back 100 metres – the back of a US
vehicle; Bottom: with BBC's John Humphrys

Top: BBC Team during the Today Programme broadcast.
Bottom: Enjoying a cheeky glass of Jacob's Creek with
Margaret Beckett

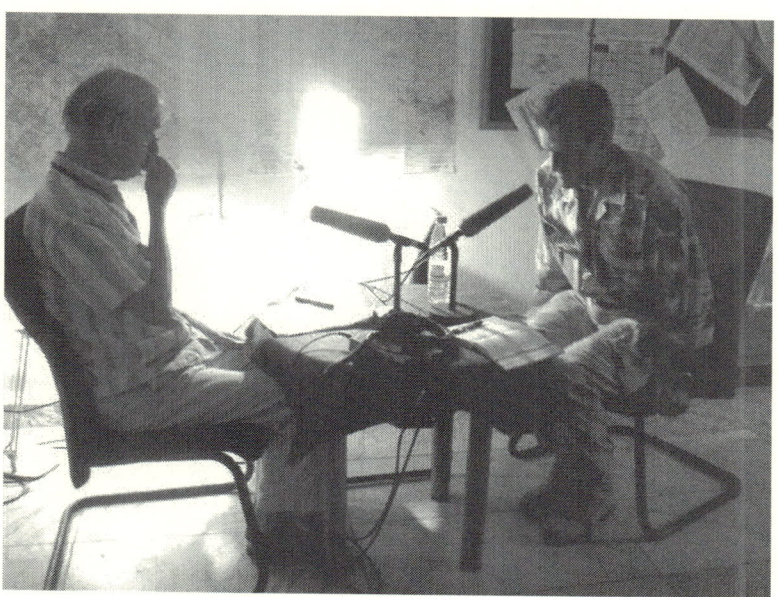

Top: Margaret Beckett stepping away from the group as she receives news from London that Tony is losing backing over his decision to stay until next spring. Heard to say, "I can't hear very well, there is a Warrior going past"; Bottom: a tense moment - General Shirreff during his Humphrys interview

Top: with Ghaith from the Guardian and the CNN team;
Bottom: A hole made by the rocket that hit Saman's
accommodation

The view across the lake (my Tai Chi spot)

Top: my pod accommodation; Bottom: The British Embassy Office in the foreground with the palace complex behind

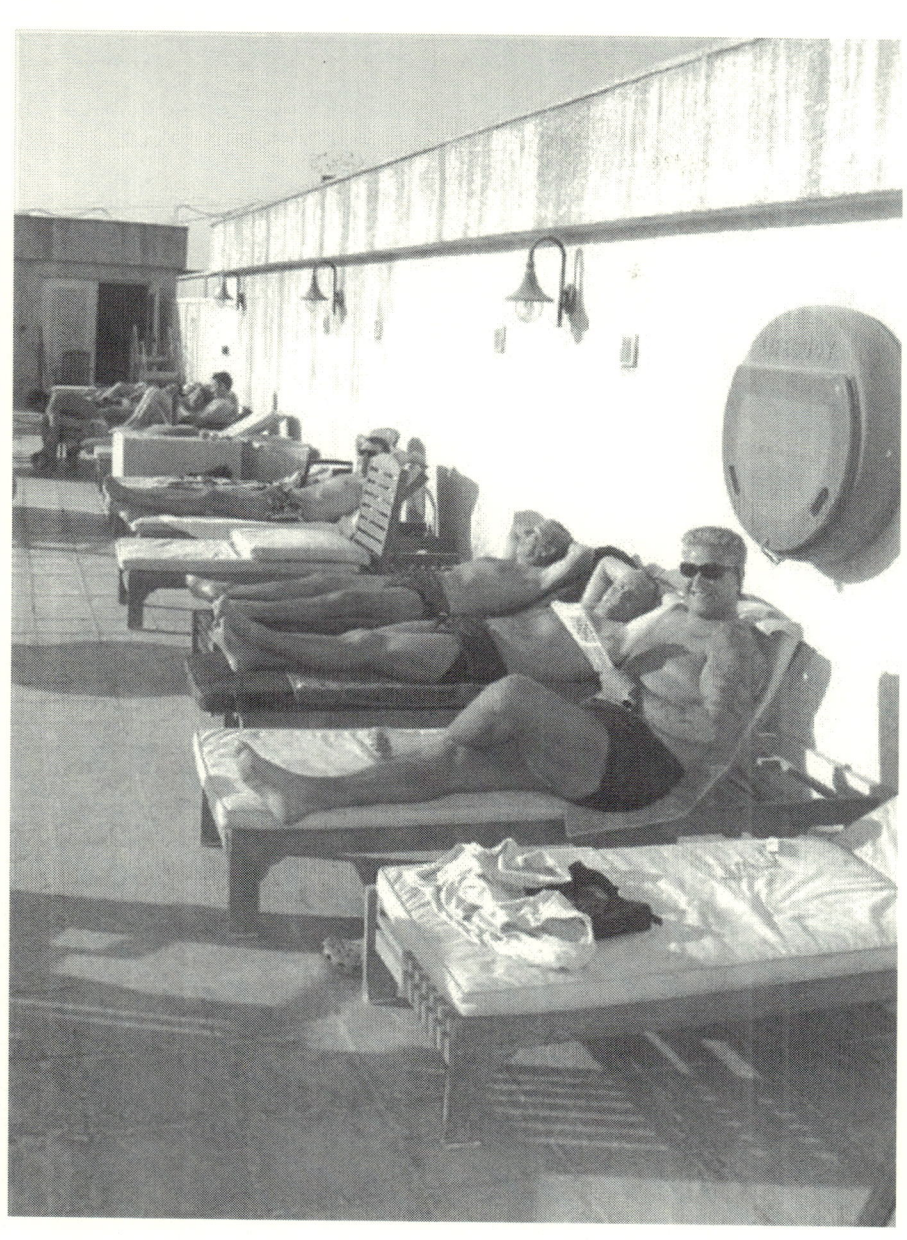

Some male colleagues relaxing by the pool

Glimpses of the real Basra – a view from a Sanger

Top: with Tash and Emma - reunited at the Air Station;
Bottom: with some of the media massive – David and Dieter

*The recovered vehicle which lost our CRG operative his leg -
being photographed by one of our medics, Chris - who was
himself an amazing photographer.*

A Portrait of John Humphrys in his live broadcast from the Palace – painted on my return in 2007

A painting of Saddam's Gate – a birthday present for Jason

ABBREIVIATIONS

AFP – Associated French Press

AP – Associated Press

COB – Central Operating Base

CPT – Close Protection Team

CG – Consul General

CRG – Control Risks Group (contractor tasked with FCO personnel security)

DFID – Department for International Development

FCO – Foreign & Commonwealth Office

HMA – Her Majesty's Ambassador

IDF – Indirect (in direct!) Fire

IED – Improvised Explosive Device (or roadside bomb)

JAM – Jaish Al Mahdi (or Al Mahdi Army)

KBR – Company contracted to provide the FCO with "life support" – cooking, cleaning, management

MOD – Ministry of Defence

NAAFI- basic supplies shop

PRT – Provincial Reconstruction Team

PTSD – Post Traumatic Stress Disorder

RPG - Rocket propelled grenade

Printed in Great Britain
by Amazon.co.uk, Ltd.,
Marston Gate.